THE LAND OF THE
PHARAOHS

T0348030

Samuel Manning's classic work is indispensable for anyone interested in the history of Egyptology. Arranged in
the form of a journey proceeding through Alexandria,
Cairo, Assouan and Abu-Simbel, the book contains a
wealth of archaeological and historical information.
Manning's prose pulses with the excitement familiar to
anyone who has ventured into unexplored territory,
whether physically or in his imagination.

KARNAK.   [*Frontispiece.*

THE LAND OF THE

PHARAOHS

SAMUEL MANNING

LONDON AND NEW YORK

First published in 2004 by
Kegan Paul International

This edition first published in 2011 by
Routledge
2 Park Square, Milton Park, Abingdon, Oxfordshire OX14 4RN

Simultaneously published in the USA and Canada
by Routledge
711 Third Avenue, New York, NY 10017

First issued in paperback 2014

Routledge is an imprint of the Taylor and Francis Group, an informa business

© Kegan Paul, 2004

British Library Cataloguing in Publication Data
A catalogue record for this book is available from the British Library

ISBN 13: 978-0-7103-0986-0 (hbk)
ISBN 13: 978-0-415-64956-8 (pbk)

Publisher's Note
The publisher has gone to great lengths to ensure the quality of this reprint
but points out that some imperfections in the original copies may be
apparent. The publisher has made every effort to contact original copyright
holders and would welcome correspondence from those they have been
unable to trace.

PREFACE TO THE NEW EDITION

D R. MANNING'S book is too well known, and has proved its worth too conclusively, to stand in need of any lengthy introduction; and the object of this preface is simply to explain to the reader the form in which it now appears.

Its remarkably vivacious record of travel presents a picture of an Egypt which is rapidly passing away, and which in a few years will have entirely ceased to exist, while its place is taken by the modern, self-governed Egypt, which may or may not be more prosperous and contented, but will certainly be a great deal less picturesque.

Dr. Manning's Egypt is the land where the Khedive Ismail, that attractive spendthrift, was still taking no thought for the morrow, and piling up liabilities in a fashion which eventually brought about his own deposition, and, incidentally, the British occupation; the land where everything was the reverse of what it ought to be, and would be anywhere else; the land where Mariette ruled at the Service of Antiquities with an iron hand, and where the idea of the wonders which might be revealed by adequate modern excavation was only beginning to glimmer on the horizon.

To attempt any extensive alterations in a book

written in the spirit of such a time would only be to mar its charm and lower its key. Accordingly, Dr. Manning's narrative has been left practically untouched, save for a few minor corrections. Where the modern advance in knowledge has rendered any more serious modification of his statements necessary, the alteration has not been made in the text, but by means of a note embodying the facts as known at the present day. Most of these notes will be found to refer to the department of Egyptian antiquities, where the additions to our knowledge have of late years been so great.

An entirely new chapter has been written, giving a short summary of some of the more remarkable results of excavation since 1880, and there has thus been added to Dr. Manning's vivid picture of the Egypt of yesterday as much as possible of that charm of the Egypt of three millenniums ago which is finding its fullest expression in the latest work at the Tomb of Tutankhamen.

JAMES BAIKIE.

CONTENTS

SEBEK, GOD OF THE FAYUM.

LIST OF ILLUSTRATIONS

9

THE LAND
OF THE
PHARAOHS

CHAPTER I

ALEXANDRIA TO CAIRO

IN the dim grey dawn of a February morning, I was
on the deck of the Austrian steamer *Urano*, peering
eagerly through the mist to the southward. The
clear crystalline blue of the Mediterranean had changed
to a greenish grey, showing that we were in shallow water.
As the sun rose, the haze vanished, and we could make
out the coast-line, a long stretch of sand, here and there
broken by a hillock, a clump of palm-trees, an Arab
village, or the white walls and dome of a *santon's* tomb.
Then a forest of masts came into view, and, rising above
them, a venerable column and a lighthouse. The column
we recognise as Pompey's Pillar ; the lighthouse is the
modern representative of the famous Pharos of Alexandria,
one of the wonders of the ancient world. We were
approaching that mysterious land which had attained a
high civilisation, and a settled monarchy, when Abram
" went forth from Ur of the Chaldees, to go into the land
of Canaan." [1] It was in its glory when the Hebrews

[1] Genesis xi. 13.

13

were there held in bondage.   It had passed its prime when David and Solomon sat upon the throne of Israel.   It had sunk into decay when Rome rose to power, and at the dawn of modern history it had ceased to exist as a nation. Hebrew patriarchs, Greek philosophers, Persian, Macedonian, and Roman conquerors, have all been drawn hither, and its annals are inextricably interwoven with theirs.   It played an important part in the greatest event in our world's history, when Joseph " arose and took the young Child and His mother by night, and departed into Egypt : and was there until the death of Herod : that it might be fulfilled which was spoken of the Lord by the prophet, saying, Out of Egypt have I called My Son " [1]   In later ages the land of the Pharaohs is ever coming into prominence.   Amongst the early Christians, Cyril, and Athanasius, and Origen ; amongst the early Mohammedans, Amrou and Omar ; amongst the Crusaders, St. Louis of France, and Saladin, the chivalrous enemy of Richard Cœur de Lion, all lead our thoughts to Egypt.   What wonder, then, that it was with a feeling of almost reverential awe, that I first gazed upon the soil which, for four thousand years, had been the scene of so many memorable deeds ?

The gravity of those of our party who were for the first time visiting Mohammedan countries, was somewhat disturbed by the appearance of the pilot who now came alongside.   His dress was a curious combination of Eastern and Western attire, very characteristic of the mongrel population of Alexandria.   It consisted of a Turkish fez, an Arab *abba*, baggy linen knickerbockers, and a pair of unmistakable English boots with elastic

---

[1] Matthew ii. 14, 15.   Hosea xi. 1.

sides. Having seated himself cross-legged on the gang-way of the steamer, pipes and coffee were served, and he steered us through the intricate channel into the harbour of Alexandria. The usual scene of confusion now ensued. Scores of boats came round us, manned, as at Jaffa, by half-naked negroes and Arabs. I was seized by half-a-dozen fellows at once, each endeavouring to appropriate me. A similar conflict was going on over every article of my baggage, and it was only by a vigorous application of the dragoman's whip that I and my belongings were rescued from them and stowed away in one of the boats.

We only escaped from the hands of the boatmen to fall into those of the donkey-boys, who effectually dissipated whatever feelings of reverence yet remained. These Arab lads are surely the cleverest and most impudent little urchins on earth. Our city arabs cannot compare with them. In broken English they vaunt the praises of their animals : " Take my donkey ; him berry good donkey ; him name Billy Barlow." If the traveller be presumably an American, the sobriquet is changed to " Yankee Doodle." One ingenious youth, whose only garment was a ragged cotton shirt, through which his tawny skin showed conspicuously, having tried " Billy Barlow," " Champagne Charley," and half-a-dozen names besides, made a final appeal, by exclaiming, " Him name Rosher Tishburne ; him speak English ; him say, ' How you do, sar ? ' " It was impossible either to lose one's temper or retain one's gravity amid this merry, clamorous crowd. At length we extricated ourselves from them and made our way to the hotel.

Anywhere, except in Egypt, Alexandria would be regarded as a very ancient city. Its history goes back more than two thousand years, to the time of its founder, Alexander the Great, B.C. 333. But here, this venerable antiquity seems quite modern. It is a mere *parvenue*, which sprang up when the kingdom of the Pharaohs had run its course and reached its close. It is now a busy thriving port in which the East and West meet in strange confusion. Nubians, Arabs, Berbers, Greeks, Italians, French, English, Circassian pilgrims, Lascar sailors, Chinese coolies, jostle one another in the crowded streets. A string of camels pass with their burdens into the railway station. A Bedouin sheikh takes a ticket for Cairo, or wrangles over the price of a piece of Manchester goods. Hadjis from Mecca are waiting to go on board the steamer bound for Constantinople or Beirout. Sailors from the harbour, or soldiers *en route* for India, shoulder their way through the bazaars. Go into a bank or counting-house, and you might fancy yourself to be in the heart of London. Step out into the street, and you see a devout Mussulman spreading his prayer-carpet in the roadway, and performing his devotions, as little disturbed by the bustle around him as though he were alone in the desert.

The northern coast-line of Egypt is a sterile waste, consisting of little else than salt swamps, lakes of brackish water, and barren sand. The importance and prosperity of Alexandria are therefore due, not to the surrounding district, but to the fact that it is the port for the only African river which flows into the Mediterranean. Regions of boundless fertility stretch southward to the equator, through which the Nile flows and forms their sole means of communication with the sea. To the ancient world, Alexandria, which lay near the mouths of this mighty river, formed the meeting-place of Eastern

IN CAIRO.

and Western civilisation—the emporium of European, Asiatic, and African commerce. With the downfall of the Byzantine Empire, its glory departed. The Mohammedan conquest fell like a blight upon its prosperity, and the discovery of the route by the Cape of Good Hope gave the death-blow to its commerce. For many generations it was little more than an obscure village of the Turkish Empire. During the present century it has again been rising into importance. Its present population is estimated at a quarter of a million.[1] In the year 1883, its exports reached upwards of twelve millions sterling, its imports seven and a half millions. The opening of the Suez Canal diverted the through traffic to India into the new channel. But other causes have since been at work, which have more than made up for the loss thus sustained, and the population and commercial prosperity of the city are rapidly increasing.

There are few remains of the ancient splendour of the city of Alexander the Great and the Ptolemies. Pompey's Pillar and Cleopatra's Needles have no right to the names they bear. The former was erected by Pompeius, prefect of Egypt, in honour of the Emperor Diocletian (A.D. 302). The monoliths of red syenite granite, covered with hieroglyphics, known as Cleopatra's Needles, formerly stood at Heliopolis, where they were raised by Thothmes III., a Pharaoh of the eighteenth dynasty.[2] They were removed to Alexandria by one of the Cæsars, and are doubtless the same which Pliny described as standing in front of the Cæsarium. One of

[1] The population of Alexandria is now 407,256, about a quarter of this number being Europeans.
[2] The mummy of this great monarch was discovered at Deir-el-Bahari in 1881. See Section IV. of this volume, also *Cleopatra's Needle. By-paths of Bible Knowledge*, No. 1, pp. 119–121.

B

them has been removed to New York; the other, presented to the British nation by Mohammed Ali, was brought to this country and placed upon the Thames Embankment at the cost of Dr. Erasmus Wilson in 1877.

On the downfall of the Hebrew monarchy, Alexandria became a new home to the exiled Jews. They so greatly increased in wealth and numbers, that at one period they formed a third of the whole population of the city. Numerous synagogues were built in the cities of Lower Egypt, and a temple upon the plan of that at Jerusalem was erected in the nome of Heliopolis. It was for the use of these Hellenistic Jews that the Septuagint translation was made, which had so important an influence in preparing the way for the introduction of the Gospel, by making the Old Testament Scriptures known to the Gentile world. The history of this version is obscured by myth and legend. All that is known, with certainty, is that the translators were Alexandrian Jews, and that it was completed under the patronage of Ptolemy Philadelphus.

A remarkable case of deliverance from persecution, and of punishment coming upon the persecutors, is recorded of the Jewish colony at Alexandria. Ptolemy Philopator (B.C. 217), being incensed at the refusal of the high-priest to admit him into the temple at Jerusalem, returned to Egypt and cast into prison all the Jews upon whom he could lay his hands. Those of Alexandria were confined in the Hippodrome, a vast amphitheatre used for gladiatorial shows and public games. The king ordered that they should be trampled to death by elephants, made furious by wine and stimulating drugs. For two days the execution was delayed by the drunken carousals of the king. This interval was spent by the

prisoners in ceaseless prayer to God for deliverance.   On
the third day the savage beasts were driven into the arena
and urged upon the prisoners.   But, instead of attacking
them, they turned upon the guards and spectators, many
of whom were killed, the rest fleeing in terror.   Ptolemy
was so impressed by this manifestation of the Divine
power that he ordered the prisoners to be released,
restored their privileges, and, as in the days of Esther
and Ahasuerus, gave them permission to kill their
enemies.

The journey from Alexandria to Cairo is now almost
always made by railway, a distance of one hundred and
twenty-eight miles.   The road first skirts the shores of
Lake Mareotis, with myriads of pelicans, wild ducks,
and other water-fowl swimming or wading in its brackish
waters, or soaring in dense clouds overhead.   The narrow strip of desert which forms the northern coast-line
of Egypt is soon crossed, and we enter the Delta of the
Nile, which continues almost as far as Cairo.   The soil,
a deposit of Nile mud, is of extraordinary fertility.   The
Delta used to be regarded as the granary of Rome.
Innumerable vessels were employed in conveying the
wheat grown in this district to the imperial city.   In
one of these the Apostle Paul was wrecked, and in
another he completed his voyage to Italy as a prisoner.[1]
The river formerly ran through it in seven channels.
Five of these are now dried up, and two only remain,
known as the Rosetta and the Damietta branches.   The
change was foretold by the prophet Isaiah : " The Lord
shall utterly destroy the tongue of the Egyptian sea, and
with His mighty wind shall He shake His hand over the

---

[1] Acts xxvii. 6–38 ; xxviii. 11.

river, and shall smite it in the seven streams, and make men go over dryshod." [1]

It seems certain that the eastern portion of the Delta was the Land of Goshen, in which the patriarchs were settled on their coming down into Egypt. It lay between Canaan and the residence of Joseph at On, or Heliopolis, for, on receiving tidings of the arrival of his father, " Joseph made ready his chariot, and went up to meet Israel his father, to Goshen, and presented himself unto him." From the marvellous fertility of the soil, it was well suited for a pastoral people, it was " the best of the land." Though belonging to the Egyptian monarchy, and used as a pasture-ground for Pharaoh's cattle, it did not form part of Egypt Proper. Hence, it was allotted to a shepherd race, where they lived without coming into offensive contact with the native population, " for every shepherd is an abomination to the Egyptians." [2] It is probable that yet another reason for the settlement of his brethren in this frontier province suggested itself to the sagacious mind of Joseph. The nomad races of Palestine were, about this period, a serious peril to the Egyptian monarchy. The mysterious Hyksos, or shepherd kings, were a Canaanitish horde, who poured across the Isthmus, and, for a time, established themselves as conquerors in the Nile Valley. Whether this invasion had already taken place, or whether it was now an object of alarm, may be doubted. But, in either case, the location of a band of hardy and warlike herdsmen on the frontier, to bear the brunt of the first assault, was a piece of policy worthy of the wisdom of the illustrious Grand

[1] Isaiah xi. 15 ; xix. 5. The literal fulfilment of this prophecy becomes still more apparent when it is remembered that the two mouths still remaining are artificial, not natural channels.
[2] Genesis xlvi. 28–34 ; xlvii. 1–6.

Vizier, who had already saved his adopted country from the horrors of famine.

The most interesting city of this district was T'sān, which in Hebrew becomes Zoan, in Greek Tanis, and in Arabic Sān. Tanis in all probability is referred to in Numbers xiii. 22, where we read, " Now Hebron was built seven years before Zoan in Egypt," and in Psalm lxxviii. 12, " Marvellous things did He in the sight of their fathers, in the land of Egypt, in the field of Zoan." For ages it was a great and powerful city, and at one period was the chief centre of the Hyksos power. A king named Apepi III. was ruling there when Ra-Sekenen of Thebes (the recent discovery and unwrapping of whose mummy is referred to in Section IV.) led the national movement which resulted in the expulsion, eighty years afterwards, of the shepherd kings. Tanis was captured finally by Aahmes I., and the hatred felt by the Egyptians towards the foreign dynasty which had so long ruled them led them to mutilate or destroy all existing monuments of the Hyksos rule, which had extended over a period of 511 years.[1]

Until 1798 the site of Tanis was unexplored, and in that year it was only surveyed by the French engineers ; but between 1815 and 1836 many of its antiquities were carried off and sold to wealthy collectors. In

---

[1] The Hyksos domination had probably begun before the rise of Joseph. Modern historians tend to shorten considerably the period of Hyksos rule. Thus the *Cambridge Ancient History* places the invasion at 1800 B.C. and the expulsion of the invaders at 1600, while Breasted, *History of Egypt*, allows only 208 years for the whole period from the XIIIth to the XVIIth Dynasty, and affirms that " a hundred years is ample for the whole period " of Hyksos power. On the other hand, Petrie, *History of Egypt*, allows 1779 years for the period from the XIIIth to the XVIIth Dynasty, and accepts the 511 years assigned by Josephus to the Hyksos domination as quite reasonable.

1860, Mariette uncovered the temple ruins, and in so doing revealed an enormous number of most valuable remains.

In 1884, Dr. Flinders Petrie explored the site anew, under the direction of the Egypt Exploration Fund. Although productive of no exceptional discoveries, many most valuable antiquities were thus brought to light.

In 1883, the same society sent out M. Naville to explore what was then known as Tel-el-Maskhutah, and was supposed to be the site of the ancient Raamses. M. Naville claims to have proved by his excavations that the site is Pithom, the ancient store city built by the Israelites, and that it is identical with Succoth, Pithom and Succoth being only different names for the same place. These results have not been accepted as final by all Egyptologists, but they all tend to increase our knowledge of what was anciently the Land of Goshen.[1]

As the train bears us slowly, and with frequent stoppages, over the district where the sons of Jacob pastured their flocks and herds, we have abundant opportunities for observing the habits of the people. A wide expanse of verdure stretches to the very verge of the horizon. Groups of fellaheen, or peasantry, are seen sitting under the shadow of a palm-grove, or lounging by the wayside, utterly indifferent to the intense heat, which makes the atmosphere quiver like the mouth of a furnace. Veiled women, clad only in a blue cotton skirt, come down to the river to fill their water-jars, and then, poising them on

---

[1] Naville's identification of Tell el-Maskhutah with Pithom has recently been questioned by Gardiner, who maintains that the more probable site is Tell er-Retabeh, which Petrie, on the other hand, identified with Raamses. See the discussion in Peet's *Egypt and the Old Testament*, and Petrie in *Ancient Egypt*, 1923, p. 75.

their heads, walk away with a firm, graceful step. A family pass along the road ; the husband, a big, stalwart fellow, rides a donkey ; the wife, bearing a load which would be heavy for an English porter, walks by his side ; a group of brown, naked children run alongside the train, holding out their hands and crying for backsheesh, and in this cry their elders join them whenever they have an opportunity. Notwithstanding this universal begging, I saw little or no actual destitution in Egypt. The wants of the peasant are so few, and the soil is so productive, and so easily cultivated, that everybody, even the very poorest, seems to be well fed. Fuel costs nothing ; and drink, the curse of European countries, is unknown. A draught of Nile water, a handful of lentils, or a piece of bread, made like a pancake, and tough as wash-leather, are all that his necessities demand. Give him a little oil or vinegar, an onion or two, and a cup of coffee, and he feasts luxuriously. A careful observation of the condition of the fellaheen convinced me of the accuracy of Miss Martineau's remarks : " I must say that I was agreeably surprised, both this morning and throughout my travels in Egypt, by the appearance of the people. About the dirt there can be no doubt ; the dirt of both dwellings and persons, and the diseases which proceed from want of cleanliness ; but the people appeared to us, there, and throughout the country, sleek, well fed, and cheerful. I am not sure that I saw an ill-fed person in all Egypt. There is hardship enough of other kinds, abundance of misery to sadden the heart of the traveller ; but not that, so far as we saw, of want of food. I am told, and no doubt truly that this is owing to the law of the Korán, by which every man is bound to share what he has, even to the last mouthful, with his brother in need ;

but there must be enough, or nearly enough, food for all, whatever be the law of distribution. Of the progressive depopulation of Egypt for many years past, I am fully convinced ; but I am confident that a deficiency of food is not the cause, nor, as yet, a consequence. While I believe that Egypt might again, as formerly, support four times its present population, I see no reason to suppose, amidst all the misgovernment and oppression that the people suffer, that they do not raise food enough to support life and health. I have seen more emaciated and stunted, and depressed men, women, and children in a single walk in England, than I observed from end to end of the land of Egypt." [1]

Though the Delta is not so entirely rainless as many parts of the Nile Valley, yet the productiveness of the soil is mainly dependent on artificial irrigation. An attempt has been made in recent years to control the Nile supply somewhat by means of an enormous dam, called the Barrage, constructed a little below Cairo.[2] The water left by the annual inundation is stored up in canals and reservoirs, and distributed over the soil by various devices. Sometimes a large wheel is run out into the river, and turned by the force of the current. The floats of the wheel are made hollow, so as to take up a quantity of water. As they rotate, and begin to descend, the contents of each are poured out into a trench, or tank, rudely constructed on the bank.

A more common method is the sâkiyeh. In every

[1] *Eastern Life, Present and Past.* By Harriet Martineau, vol. i. p. 9.
[2] The whole irrigation system has now been transformed, and the area brought under cultivation enormously increased by the erection and subsequent heightening of the great Barrage at Aswan, and the subsidiary Barrage at Assiut.

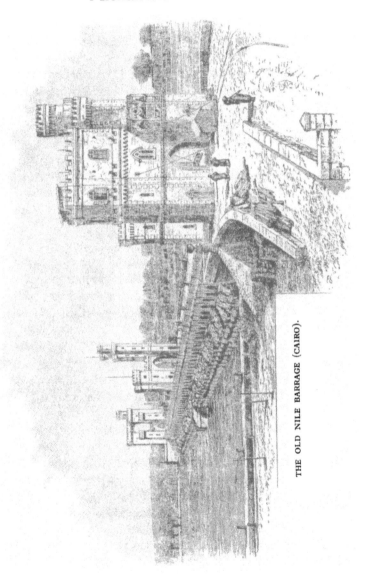

THE OLD NILE BARRAGE (CAIRO).

part of Egypt we may see a rude roof of thatch, under which a camel or buffalo plods round a worn path, turning a series of wheels cogged and creaky, drawing up an endless and dripping string of earthen vessels, which splash out their crystal gatherings into one leaky and common pool ; and thence, along a moss-clad shaft, into a little babbling rill of pure water flowing off on a bounteous errand. The groaning and creaking of these sâkiyehs is one of the most familiar sounds on the Nile. It becomes associated, in memory, with hot, sultry afternoons, spent in delicious indolence on the deck of a dahabiyeh, gliding downward with the current ; with cool evenings, when the stars come out in the deep blue of an Egyptian sky, to shine with a lustre unknown in our northern latitudes ; less pleasantly associated with restless nights, when the boat has been moored near one of these machines, and the incessant noise combines with rats, mosquitoes, fleas, and innumerable other plagues of Egypt, to banish sleep.

More common than either is the shâdûf, a primitive contrivance consisting only of a long pole working on a pivot, a lump of clay, or a stone fixed at one end, a bucket at the other. For hundreds of miles up the Nile the river is lined with these shâdûfs ; men, women, and children, either absolutely naked, or with only a strip of cloth round their loins, spending their whole lives in lifting water out of the bountiful river to irrigate their fields. No wonder that the ancient Egyptians worshipped the Nile, and that it needs all the force of Mohammedan iconoclasm to prevent the fellaheen of to-day from worshipping it too. The very existence of Egypt, as we shall see hereafter, is absolutely due to the river. Were its beneficent current to fail, or its mysterious inundation to cease, Egypt would again become a part of the desert from which it has been reclaimed, and which hems it in on either hand.

The distribution of water over the soil is effected by means of trenches leading into small channels, these again into yet smaller gutters. Each plot of land is divided into squares by ridges of earth a few inches in height. The cultivator uses his feet to regulate the flow of water to each part. By a dexterous movement of his toes, he forms a tiny embankment in one of the trenches, or removes the obstruction, or makes an aperture in one of the ridges, or closes it up again, as the condition of the crop requires. He is thus able to irrigate each square yard of his land with the utmost nicety, giving to it just as much or as little water as he thinks fit. This mode of cultivation is very ancient, and was probably referred to by Moses, when, contrasting the copious rainfall and numerous fountains of Palestine with the laborious irrigation of Egypt, he said, " For the land, whither thou goest in to possess it, is not as the land of Egypt, from whence ye came out, where thou sowedst thy seed, and *wateredst it with thy foot*, as a garden of herbs : but the land, whither ye go to possess it, is a land of hills and valleys, and drinketh water of the rain of heaven." [1]

Though the trains on Egyptian railways are probably the slowest and most irregular in the world,[2] yet some progress is made, and, in the course of a few hours, it becomes evident that our destination cannot be far distant. The broad expanse of verdure narrows as the Delta approaches its southern apex at Cairo. The tawny line of desert which bounds it on either side draws nearer.

[1] Deuteronomy xi. 10, 11.
[2] The Egyptian Railway Service no longer deserves this reproach.

The Libyan and Mokattam ranges of hills, which inclose the Nile Valley, come into view. Then, those who know where to look for them, may make out, through the quivering haze, at a distance of ten or twelve miles, the most extraordinary group of buildings in the world. In approaching almost any other object of interest for the first time—St. Peter's at Rome, for instance, or Mont Blanc—there is a brief interval of hesitation and doubt before its definite recognition. But at the very first glance, without a moment's pause, we exclaim, *The Pyramids!* They are at once the vastest and the oldest buildings on the earth. They were standing, perhaps were even already ancient, when Abraham came down into Egypt. Their origin was lost in the recesses of a remote and legendary past, when the Father of History conversed with the priests of Saïs and Memphis. It may have been bombast, but it was scarcely exaggeration, when Napoleon, on the eve of the Battle of the Pyramids, issued his famous *ordre du jour*, " Soldiers, forty centuries are looking down on you ! " And now, by a strange anachronism, we are gazing quietly out of the window of a railway carriage, at edifices which seem to be nearly coeval with the existence of man upon the earth.

But our reveries are broken in upon by our arrival at the railway station, where a struggle like that at Alexandria awaits us with the *hammals* and donkey-boys contending for the possession of our persons and baggage. Having extricated ourselves from their clutches with some difficulty, we make our way to the hotel.

Cairo lies at the entrance of the Nile Valley, near the point at which the river branches out into the channels which form the Delta. Its modern name is a European corruption of that given to it by its Arab conquerors—

El Kahira, the victorious. By the natives it is called *Misr* or *Masr*, and the same name is given by them to the whole of Egypt. This is evidently a modern form of the Scriptural Mizraim, and affords another instance of the survival of ancient names through a long course of centuries, and after repeated conquests by foreign nations.[1] It is situated about a mile from the river. A long straggling street leads down to Bûlâk, which is the port ; and Fostat, or Old Cairo, runs along the Nile bank. The population of the city was given in the census of 1882 as 374,838, but good authorities reckon it as 400,000 in round numbers. The resident Europeans amount to 21,000.[2]

Those who wish to see the Cairo of romance, and of the *Arabian Nights' Entertainments*, should lose no time in visiting it, for it is being rapidly " improved off the face of the earth." The new quarter is but a shabby repro- duction of modern Paris, from which all characteristic Oriental features—the graceful lattice-work windows, the overhanging stories, the picturesque colour—have disappeared. The Ezbekîyeh Garden has nothing but its semi-tropical vegetation to distinguish it from the public gardens of any European capital. Young Egypt, sallow-faced, and dressed in fez cap, baggy, ill-fitting black clothes, and patent leather boots, unsuccessfully affects the airs, and only too successfully cultivates the vices, of Parisian *flâneurs*. Said Pasha, who died in 1863, greatly benefited Egypt by his administrative skill and enlightened policy ; but since his day the old picturesque life of the East has been fast passing away, and a thin veneer of European civilisation has been

[1] See for numerous parallel instances *Those Holy Fields*, p. 89.
[2] The population of Cairo is now 715,609, about 60,000 being Europeans.

superimposed upon unalloyed native barbarism. That the sanitary condition of the city was horrible, and that improvement was urgently needed, cannot be questioned. If the Khedive had set himself to effect the necessary reforms by developing a system of architecture in harmony with the habits of the people, the requirements of the climate, and the characteristics of Arabian art, he would have done a good work. But the new Boulevards satisfy none of these requirements. They are simply poor imitations of a faulty original. And this applies to the whole system of administration. It is an exotic which has no roots in the soil, and no adaptation to surrounding conditions.

But, as an American gentleman said to me, " Cairo is a big place, and can stand a great deal of improving." In a few minutes we may pass from the Frank quarter into the labyrinthine windings of bazaars, which are almost unchanged since the days of Saladin, and in which " Haroun Alraschid, Giaffar, the Grand Vizier, and Mesrour, the chief of the eunuchs," might have wandered and found little to surprise them. The Muski affords us a good line of transition from the one to the other. We enter the main thoroughfare, broad for an Eastern city, with a Bavarian *bier-halle* at one corner, and at the other a shop for the sale of French books and photographs. The roadway is, of course, unpaved, but it is wide enough to allow a carriage to drive along it, with space for foot-passengers on either side. Each carriage is preceded by its running footmen—lithe, agile fellows, who can keep ahead of the horses, going at full speed, for an incredible distance. They wear a light dress of white linen, which leaves the arms and legs bare. Each carries a wand by day, a

THE BRASS BAZAAR.

flambeau by night. Their duty is to warn pedestrians to get out of the way, which they do by incessant cries : " To the right." " To the left.' " Look out in front," mingled with good-humoured abuse of those who are slow to take their warnings. Lines of camels with their long swaying necks, soft, silent tread, and peevish groans, stalk solemnly along the middle of the roadway. A string of donkeys, surmounted by inflated balloons of black silk or white muslin, from which dainty little slippers of red or yellow morocco leather peep out, are carrying the ladies of a harem to take the air. Here comes a procession of blind men chanting the Korán, followed by a group of women wailing and crying in tones of well-simulated grief ; between them is a board carried on men's shoulders and covered by a pall, beneath whose folds it is easy to make out the rigid lines of a corpse on its way to the cemetery. Shrill gurgling cries fall upon the ear, taken up and repeated by the female bystanders, perhaps with the accompaniment of a haut-boy and a drum or two. It is a marriage procession. The bride, a mere child ten or twelve years of age, swathed from head to foot in red or yellow shawls, and inclosed in a canopy or tent, is being conducted to the bath or to her husband's house.[1] Veiled women, black slaves, Bedouin sheikhs, burly pashas, water-carriers, blind beggars, Greek and Coptic priests, donkeys and their drivers, and street-sellers innumerable, make up the picturesque and bewildering throng.

The street-sellers in their number and variety would

---

[1] I saw a curious illustration in the streets of Cairo of the irresistible innovations of the West, and the unchanging customs of the East. The bride was being taken home in a *cab*, but the canopy was tied over the roof, and fixed to the four corners, to represent the four poles which usually support it.

demand a chapter to do them justice ; and to interpret
their cries requires a far greater knowledge of Arabic
than I possess.   They form, however, so important and
characteristic a feature in the aspect of an Eastern city,
that they cannot be altogether passed over.   I avail
myself, therefore, of Mr. Lane's help in the matter.
" The cries of some of the hawkers are curious, and
deserve to be mentioned.   The seller of ' tirmis ' (or
lupins) often cries, ' Aid ! O Imbábee ! Aid ! '   This
is understood in two senses ; as an invocation for aid
to the sheikh El-Imbábee, a celebrated Muslim saint,
buried at the village of Imbábeh, on the west bank of
the Nile, opposite Cairo, in the neighbourhood of which
village the best tirmis is grown ; and also as implying
that it is through the aid of the saint above-mentioned
that the tirmis of Imbábeh is so excellent.   The seller
of this vegetable also cries, ' The tirmis of Imbábeh
surpasses the almond.'   Another cry of the seller of
tirmis is, ' O how sweet the little offspring of the river ! '
The seller of sour limes cries, ' God make them light '
(or easy of sale).   The toasted pips of a kind of melon
called ' abdalláwee,' and of the water-melon, are often
announced by the cry of ' O consoler of the embarrased !
O pips ! '   A curious cry of the seller of a kind of sweetmeat (' haláweh '), composed of treacle fried with some
other ingredient, is, ' For a nail, O sweetmeat ! '   He is
said to be half a thief ; children and servants often
steal implements of iron, etc., from the house in which
they live, and give them to him in exchange for his
sweetmeat.   The hawker of oranges cries, ' Honey !
O oranges ! honey ! '   And similar cries are used by
the sellers of other fruit and vegetables, so that it is
sometimes impossible to guess what the person announces

INTERIOR OF THE MOSQUE OF THE SULTAN HASSAN.

for sale, as when we hear the cry of ' Sycamore-figs !
O grapes ! ' except by the rule that what is for sale
is the least excellent of the fruits, etc., mentioned ; as
sycamore-figs are not as good as grapes. A very singular
cry is used by the sellers of roses : ' The rose was a
thorn ; from the sweat of the Prophet it blossomed.'
This alludes to a miracle related of the Prophet. The
fragrant flowers of the henna-tree are carried about for
sale, and the seller cries, ' Odours of Paradise ! O
flowers of the henna ! ' A kind of cotton-cloth, made
by machinery which is put in motion by a bull, is
announced by the cry of ' The work of the bull ! O
maidens ! ' "

A familiar cry in the streets of Cairo is that of the
water-carrier. Sometimes he uses almost the very
words of the prophet Isaiah : " O ye thirsty, water ! "
He does not, however, go on to say, " without money
and without price ; " [1] but for a small coin, less than
an English farthing, he fills one of the brass cups which
he chinks incessantly as he walks along. A more
ambiguous cry, but one in common use is, " Oh, may
God compensate me ! " More frequently he exclaims,
" The gift of God ! " recalling the words of our Lord,
speaking to the Samaritan woman of the Holy Spirit :
" If thou knewest *the gift of God*, and who it is that
saith to thee, Give Me to drink ; thou wouldest have
asked of Him, and He would have given thee living
water." [2]

As we leave the Muski behind us, and enter the
purely native quarter, the streets become narrower, till
at length a laden camel can scarcely pass, its burden
touching the wall on either side. The upper stories of

---

[1] Isaiah lv. 1.   [2] John iv. 10.

the houses, which project as they ascend, almost meet overhead, leaving only a narrow strip of sky visible. But even yet we have not penetrated into the innermost arcana of the bazaars. I was several days searching for the goldsmiths' bazaar before I could find it. At length, passing out of a very narrow street, through a dark and filthy archway, I found myself in a gloomy passage, in which it was impossible for two persons to walk abreast. On either side the goldsmiths were busy, each with his charcoal fire, blowpipe, and anvil, producing the exquisite jewellery for which Cairo is so justly famous. Filigree work, fine as the finest lace, jewelled necklaces and nose rings, head-dresses inlaid with diamonds and pearls, were offered for sale, in dirty holes and corners, by men black with the smoke of the forge at which they had been working. There was no display of wealth. Every article was brought out separately, and its price fixed by weight. Yet even here the intrusive West had made its way. Each jeweller had at the back of his forge an iron safe made in London or Birmingham, in which his treasures were stored.

The mosques in Cairo are very numerous, not fewer, it is said, than four hundred. Many of them are of considerable size and architectural merit. But, with the single exception of that of Mohammed Ali, recently erected, they are all falling into dilapidation.[1] Many reasons are assigned for their ruinous condition. It is said that the Egyptians are deterred from repairing them by superstitious feelings. Others ascribe the neglect to a decay of religious faith and zeal. The more probable explanation is, that the government having confiscated

[1] The restoration and maintenance of the Mosques is now attended to by the *Comité de Conservation des Monuments de l'Art Arabe*.

the estates of the mosques, as well as those of private
individuals, now fail to discharge the duty of keeping
the edifices in repair. The mosque of Sultan Tooloon
is interesting to architects from the fact that, although
built a thousand years ago (A.D. 879), it had pointed
arches at least three hundred years before their introduction into England. That of Sultan Hassan, near
the citadel, is a building of great beauty, constructed
out of the casing stones of the Great Pyramid. " It
abounds," says Fairholt, " with the most enriched
details of ornament within and without ; not the least
remarkable of its fittings being the rows of coloured glass
lamps hanging from its walls, of Syrian manufacture,
bearing the Sultan's name, amid glowing coloured
decorations ; they are some of the finest early glass-
work of their kind, but many are broken, and others
hanging unsafely from half-corroded chains." Though
this mosque is the boast and pride of the Cairenes, yet
it is allowed to remain in a condition of filth and dilapidation which seems to prove that all religious zeal is
dying out from the hearts of the people.

The suburbs of Cairo, and the surrounding district,
are very interesting. Weeks may be spent in visiting
and revisiting the many points of attraction. In the
environs are charming villas, each standing in a garden,
rich in all the products of a semi-tropical country, and
abundantly supplied with water. As we ramble in the
outskirts of the city, we often come upon an open space
occupied as a fair. How like, and yet how unlike, an
English fair ! Swings and round-abouts are here, but
dark-skinned, bright-eyed Arab youngsters have taken
the place of our " young hopefuls." Yonder is a serpent-
charmer with necklace and girdle of snakes ; before

him are half a dozen puff-adders, erect upon their tails, and waving to and fro with a rhythmic motion to the music of a rude guitar. Near him sits a story-teller, reciting in guttural Arabic some interminable tale from the *Thousand and One Nights*, the group seated round him listening with a fixed attention which nothing seems to weary. Jugglers, mountebanks, and acrobats are performing their feats precisely as we see them at home. Booths, constructed with a few poles and rafters, over which a vine has been trained, afford shadow to loungers, who sit hour after hour, sipping coffee or sherbet, and listening to the dismal tones of a *tarabookah*, or Nubian drum, a reed pipe, and a dulcimer. It is a merry, and yet a sad scene. These men are mere children, with no occupation for the present ; no care, or purpose, or hope, for the future.

Continuing our ramble along the banks of the Nile, we cross a branch of the river to visit the Nilometer. It was built in the year 716 A.D. by order of the Caliph Suleiman, and has been restored many times since that date. A pit lined with masonry is sunk to the level of the bed of the river, but the lower part is choked with mud and with the remains of the dome, which has fallen in.[1] A graduated column rises in the centre indicating in cubits the height to which the inundation reaches. The sixteenth cubit is called the Sultan's water, as the land tax is only levied when this height is attained. It is notorious that the official and the true record never agree. " A good Nile," as it is called, is from eighteen to twenty-two cubits. Less than this leaves the soil insufficiently irrigated ; more than this drowns the country and inflicts immense mischief upon the peasantry. Every morning

[1] The Nilometer was restored in 1893.

THE NILOMETER.

during the rise of the river criers go throughout Cairo proclaiming the level to which the inundation has reached. The announcement is awaited with intense and eager interest, for upon it depends the question whether the coming year shall be one of famine or of abundance. When the proper height has been attained the dams are cut, allowing the water to flow into the canals, and universal rejoicings prevail throughout the city.

Perhaps there is no place in the immediate vicinity of the city which is visited and revisited with deeper interest than the Citadel. It stands on a rocky eminence which rises to the east of Cairo, and commands a magnificent view extending over the city, the desert, and far down the Nile Valley. In this wonderful view the Pyramids form the most impressive feature. Though clearly visible and within easy reach, they stand quite apart from the surrounding landscape. The narrow strip of cultivated soil along the banks of the river approaches, but does not touch, them. The solitude and silence of the desert broods over them. The noise from the city at our feet falls upon our ears. Its busy life moves beneath our eyes. But nothing breaks in upon the sense of awful mystery and separation from the existing world which invests these venerable monuments of antiquity.

A tragic interest attaches to one of the courts of the Citadel. In 1811 Mohammed Ali learned that the Mamelukes intended to rebel against him. He therefore invited their chiefs to be present in the Citadel on the investiture of his son Toossoom Pasha with the command of the army. Upwards of 400 came. The ceremony over, on mounting their horses to ride away, they found the gates closed. At the same moment, a fierce fire of musketry was opened upon them from the windows of the surrounding barracks. Resistance and escape were alike impossible. They galloped round the narrow inclosure, seeking in vain to find a way of escape or an enemy whom they might attack. Men and horses fell in heaps in the courtyard. Only one of them, Emin Bey, survived. He leaped his horse over the precipice which forms the western front of the Citadel. The animal was killed by the fall, but he escaped as by a miracle, and reached a camp of Arnauts in the plain below, who refused to surrender him to the Pasha ; and he succeeded in making his way from the country in disguise. The soldiers who had taken part in the massacre were rewarded by being permitted to plunder the houses of their victims and to complete the extermination of the Mamelukes by slaughtering those who had not been present at the ceremony. Upwards of twelve hundred are said to have perished. As we visit the splendid Mosque of Mohammed Ali, close to the scene of the massacre, it is impossible not to remember with horror this frightful tragedy.

Though few or none of the remains of the Egypt of the Pharaohs are to be found in Cairo, yet it stands in close proximity to some of the most important cities of the ancient dynasties. The site of Memphis, which we shall visit on our journey up the Nile, is only a few miles to the south. Heliopolis is still nearer. Passing out from the city, and leaving the Citadel and the tombs of the Caliphs on our right, the road leads, under avenues of tamarisk and acacia, through a richly cultivated district. Soon, however, the limits of vegetation are reached, and we enter upon the vast tract of sand which bounds Egypt on every side. The line of fertility and barrenness is

not, however, continuous and unbroken. Wherever a
depression in the soil or an extension of irrigation brings
the waters of the Nile to a point in advance of the ordinary
limit of cultivation, there the desert " rejoices and
blossoms as the rose." In one of these projecting points
of fertile soil, immediately before we reach the site of
the ancient city, is a garden, in the midst of which stands
a venerable sycamore tree, hollow, gnarled, and almost
leafless with extreme age. It is enclosed by palisades,
and is regarded with veneration by the Copts as the place
where Joseph, Mary, and the infant Saviour rested on
their flight into Egypt. The fact that there was a great
Jewish settlement in this neighbourhood gives a certain
measure of plausibility to the legend. The tree itself,
though evidently of great age, cannot be as ancient as
the legend affirms.[1]

The road now leads through a wide plain, covered
with a luxuriant growth of sugar-cane. From amidst
the broad green glossy leaves a single column of red
granite rises, covered from summit to base with hieroglyphics. It is the sole relic above the soil of the once
famous City of the Sun—the Heliopolis of Herodotus
and Strabo, the Bethshemesh of Jeremiah,[2] the On of
Joseph.[3] To this great university city of ancient Egypt,
Plato, Eudoxus, and the wisest of the Greeks, came to
be initiated into the mystic lore of the priests. Here,
as Manetho tells us, Moses was instructed in all " the
learning of the Egyptians." This solitary column,
raised about a century before the time of Joseph, looked
down on his marriage with " Asenath, the daughter of
Potipherah." It has stood in its present position for

[1] This tree succumbed to old age in 1906. It was planted in
1672, on the site of an earlier tree, which died in 1665.
[2] Jeremiah xliii. 13.   [3] Genesis xli. 45.

nearly four thousand years, and is the sole survivor of the avenues of sphinxes, the temples and palaces, and colleges and obelisks, described by Greek historians. Even in Egypt we shall visit few spots invested with a deeper and more various interest than this.

But the great excursion from Cairo yet awaits us— that to the Pyramids. I had seen them so frequently from a distance, and had been so deeply impressed by their solemn and solitary grandeur, that it was with an apprehension of disappointment that I started in the early morning to spend a long day in examining them more closely. Until recently, the trip was not without some difficulty. The Nile had to be crossed by a ferry ; donkeys were the only means of conveyance ; and the traveller must often go some miles out of his way to avoid a canal or a tract of land under water, or he must be carried over it on men's shoulders. Now a noble bridge is thrown across the river, and a broad highway, above the reach of the inundation, leads under an avenue of carob trees, past the Khedive's palace, to the very foot of the plateau on which the Pyramids stand. Lovers of romance and adventure complain of the change, and they hear with dismay that a branch railway is talked of.[1] It is certainly a very prosaic affair to drive out to Gîzeh in a carriage and pair, with as little risk or trouble as is involved in a trip to Richmond. But for those who have only a single day to devote to the excursion, the new road is not without its advantages.

In about an hour after leaving the Ezbekiyeh, we see

[1] Lovers of romance have now to submit to the fact that an electric tramway runs hourly to the Mena House Hotel, beside the Pyramids, with an extra service at Full Moon, to allow of tourists visiting the spot by moonlight. Perhaps the moonlight service may be regarded as some mitigation of the offence !

THE SPHINX.

the Pyramids rising from the sandy plain, evidently close at hand. The first view is certainly disappointing. They are much smaller, and also much nearer, than we had supposed. Two hours was the time allotted for the journey thither, yet our watches show that only one has passed. We soon discover that we are under an optical illusion. The perfect clearness of the air, the want of any intervening objects to break the monotony of the plain, or to mark the distance, and the immense size of the Pyramids themselves, had led us to suppose that we had reached our destination when less than half of the distance had been traversed. As we sped on our way, they loomed larger and larger before us, till at length, when we found ourselves at the foot of the plateau, they fully realised all our expectations. I, at least, felt nothing of the disappointment and disenchantment to which many travellers have given expression.

Vast and imposing as are the Pyramids even at the present day, it is important to remember that we do not see them in their original condition. It has been said that, " All things dread Time ; but Time itself dreads the Pyramids." The destructive agency of man, how-ever, has effected what mere natural decay was powerless to accomplish. The huge masses of masonry are indeed proof against the assaults alike of man and of time. But as originally constructed, they offered not the rough and broken outline up which we now climb, but a smooth and polished surface, perhaps covered with hieroglyphics. For centuries they furnished quarries out of which modern Egyptians have built their cities. Though their beauty has been thus destroyed, their bulk is not per-ceptibly diminished. Abd-el-Atif, an Arab physician, writing in the twelfth century, when the casing stones

were yet in their places, says : " The most admirable
particular of the whole is the extreme nicety with which
these stones have been prepared and adjusted. Their
adjustment is so precise that not even a needle or a hair
can be inserted between any two of them. They are
joined by a cement laid on to the thickness of a sheet of
paper. These stones are covered with writing in that
secret character whose import is at this day wholly
unknown. These inscriptions are so multitudinous,
that if only those which are seen on the surface of these
two Pyramids were copied upon paper, more than ten
thousand books would be filled with them." One of
these inscriptions is said by Herodotus to have recorded
that sixteen hundred talents of silver were expended in
purchasing radishes, onions, and garlic for the workmen ;
reminding us of the complaint of the Israelites : " We
remember the fish, which we did eat in Egypt freely ;
the cucumbers, and the melons, and the leeks, and the
onions, and the garlic." [1]

If, as we stand upon the plateau of Gîzeh, now covered
with mounds of ruin and débris, we would picture to
ourselves the scene which it presented in the time of the
Pharaohs, we must conceive of the three Pyramids as
huge masses of highly-polished granite,[2] the area around

[1] In spite of the statements of Herodotus and Abd-el-Atif, there
can be no doubt that the Pyramids of Gîzeh never bore hieroglyphic
inscriptions. The inscribed pyramids are those of the Kings Unas,
Teti, Pepy I., Merenra, and Pepy II., of the Vth and VIth Dynasties,
at Saqqara. These were opened by Maspero in 1880, when the
" Pyramid Texts," which have proved of supreme value in the study
of early Egyptian religion, were discovered.

[2] The Great Pyramid and the Second Pyramid were not cased
with granite, but with limestone. The Third Pyramid was cased
with red granite to a height of sixteen courses from its base ; but the
upper casing, in this instance also, was of limestone. Granite was
used freely in all three pyramids for interior work which was meant
to be specially sumptuous, and even for a single course, the lowest,

them covered with pyramids and temples, amongst which
the Sphinx rose in solemn, awful grandeur to a height of

ENTRANCE TO THE GREAT PYRAMID.

a hundred feet. What is now a silent waste of desert

of the Second Pyramid ; but the whole construction is essentially
of limestone.

Each Pyramid was the centre of a complex of building, consisting
of the Pyramid itself, the Pyramid-Temple, where offerings were
made to the dead king, the causeway, leading down to the edge of the
high Nile, and the Portico-Temple, which stood at the lower end
of the causeway. The so-called "Temple of the Sphinx," which
was discovered by Mariette in 1853, is really the Portico-Temple of
the Second Pyramid.

sand would be thronged with priests, and nobles, and soldiers, in all the pomp and splendour with which the monuments make us familiar, while just below us, stretching along the Nile, the palaces of Memphis glittered in the sun. As we realise to ourselves this magnificent spectacle, we may understand something of the self-denial manifested by Moses when " he refused to be called the son of Pharaoh's daughter ; " and of his dauntless courage when he stood before the king, and demanded that he should " let the people go." It was only as " by faith he endured, as seeing Him who is invisible," that he was able to rise to this height of heroism ; " choosing rather to suffer affliction with the people of God, than to enjoy the pleasures of sin for a season ; esteeming the reproach of Christ greater riches than the treasures in Egypt: for he had respect unto the recompence of the reward." [1]

The following are the dimensions of these stupendous monuments :

	1st Pyramid.		2nd Pyramid.		3rd Pyramid.	
	Present.	Original.	Present.	Original.	Present.	Original.
	Feet.	Feet.	Feet.	Feet.	Feet.	Feet.
Sides of the base : . .	750	768	690¼	707½	356¼	356¼
Slant height . . .	568	610	563¾	572¼	263¾	279¾
Perpendicular height .	451	482	447½	454	204	219
Angle of elevation . .	51°50°	—	52°20°	—	51°	—

The Great Pyramid is, therefore, more than half as long again on every side as Westminster Abbey, and, though deprived of more than thirty feet by the removal of its apex, it is still fifty feet higher than the top of St. Paul's, and more than twice as high as the central tower of York Minster. It covers thirteen acres of ground, equal to the area of Lincoln's Inn Fields, and is

[1] Heb. xi. 14–27.

computed to have contained 6,848,000 tons of solid masonry.

The pyramid itself contains two chambers, which have received the appellation of the *King's* and *Queen's*. The latter is lined with slabs of polished stone, very carefully finished, and artistically roofed with blocks

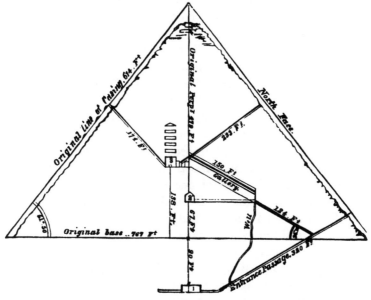

SECTION OF THE GREAT PYRAMID FROM NORTH TO SOUTH.
1. SUBTERRANEAN VAULT   2. QUEEN'S CHAMBER.   3. KING'S CHAMBER.

leaning against each other to resist the pressure of the mass above. This apartment is reached by a sloping passage, which terminates in a gallery or hall twenty-eight feet high. From the entrance to the gallery a horizontal passage, one hundred and nine feet long, leads to the "queen's chamber," which measures seventeen feet (north and south) by eighteen wide, and is twenty feet high to the top of the inclined blocks.

The gallery continues to ascend till it reaches a sort of vestibule, which leads to the "king's chamber." This chamber is finished with as much care as the other, and measures thirty-four feet by seventeen, and nineteen in height. The north and south walls are pierced by two shafts or tubes, about eight inches square, slanting up through the entire fabric to the exterior of the pyramid.

The "king's chamber" contained a red granite sarcophagus without a lid ; it was empty, and had neither sculpture nor inscription of any kind. The door was guarded by a succession of four heavy stone portcullises, intended to be let down after the body was deposited, and impenetrably seal up the access. The roof of the chamber is flat ; and, in order to take off the weight above, five spaces, or *entresols*, have been left in the structure. On the wall of one of these garrets, never intended to be entered, General Vyse discovered, in 1836, what had been searched for in every other part of the pyramid in vain. Drawn in red ochre, apparently as quarry marks on the stones previously to their insertion, are several hieroglyphic characters, among which is seen the oval ring which encircles the royal titles, and within it a name which had already been noticed on an adjoining tomb. On the latter it was read *Khufu*, a word sufficiently near, in the Egyptian pronunciation, to *Cheops*, whom Herodotus gives as the founder of the largest pyramid.

Cartouche of Cheops.

One of the most singular features in this pyramid is a perpendicular shaft descending from the gallery in front of the " queen's chamber " down to the entrance passage underground, a depth of 155 feet. The work-manship shows that this well was sunk through the masonry *after* the completion of the pyramid, in all probability as an outlet for the masons, after barring the sloping ascent with a mass of granite on the inside, which long concealed its existence. The lower opening of the well was closed with a similar stone ; the builders then withdrawing by the northern entrance, which was both barricaded and concealed under the casing, left the interior, as they supposed, inaccessible to man.

These extraordinary precautions go to confirm the tradition related by Herodotus, that Cheops was not buried in the vault he had prepared, but secretly in some safer retreat, on account of violence apprehended from the people.[1] As no other pyramid is known to contain an upper room, it seems not improbable that the " queen's chamber " was the refuge where his mummy lay con-cealed while the vault was broken open and searched in vain.

Lepsius has shown that the Pyramids were con-structed by degrees. The vault was excavated, and a course of masonry laid over it, in the first year of the king's reign. If he died before a second was completed, the corpse was interred, and the pyramid built up solid above. With every year of the king's life an addition was made to the base as well as to the superstructure, so that the years of the reign might have been numbered by the accretions, as the age of a tree by its annual rings. When the last year came, the steps were filled out to a plane surface, the casing put on, and the royal corpse conveyed through the slanting passage to its resting-place.[2]

---

[1] This idea is devoid of foundation.
[2] The theory of Lepsius was controverted by Petrie, who as the

The Second Pyramid stands about 500 feet to the south-west of the First, and is so placed that the diagonals of both are in a right line. It is somewhat smaller, but stands on higher ground. The construction is similar to the other, save that no chamber has been discovered above ground. It was surrounded by a pavement, through which a second entrance, in front of the northern face, descends deep into the rock, and then rises again to meet the usual passage from the regular opening in the face of the pyramid. From the point of junction a horizontal passage leads to a vault, now called by the name of Belzoni; it measures forty-six feet by sixteen, and is twenty-two feet in height. It is entirely hewn in the rock, with the exception of the roof, which is formed of vast limestone blocks, leaning against each other and painted inside. When discovered, this vault contained a plain granite sarcophagus, without inscription, sunk into the floor. The lid was half destroyed, and it was full of rubbish. Some bones found in the interior turned out to be the remains of oxen; but the sarcophagus was not large enough to admit more than a human mummy. Besides the large vault, Belzoni found a smaller one, eleven feet long, and a third, measuring thirty-four feet by ten, and eight feet five in height, but neither contained any sepulchral remains.

The general workmanship of this pyramid is inferior to that of the larger one. It retains its outer casing for about 150 feet from the top, and is, consequently, more difficult of ascent. No name has been found on any

result of his researches maintained that each pyramid was planned from the beginning on the scale on which it was afterwards completed. Borchardt, however, has since revived the theory of Lepsius with modifications; but the idea is difficult to reconcile with the known length of the reigns of some of the pyramid-builders.

THE CEMETERY AND TOMBS OF THE CALIPHS, CAIRO.

part of the Second Pyramid, and its erection is not
mentioned by Manetho. A tradition preserved by
Diodorus assigned it to Amasis ; but an ad-
jacent tomb contains an inscription to a royal
architect, in which the monarch is called
" Khafra the Great of the Pyramid," and this
has been supposed to be Chephren, the brother
of Cheops, to whom Herodotus ascribes the
Second Pyramid.

Cartouche of Chephren.

The Third or Red Pyramid—so called from the
colour of the granite casing which covered the lower
half, and has protected its base from diminution—is
described by the classical writers as the most sumptuous
and magnificent of all. It certainly surpasses the other
two in beauty and regularity of construction.[1] It covers
a suite of three subterranean chambers, reached as usual
by a sloping passage from the northern face. The first
is an anteroom twelve feet long, the walls panelled in
white stucco. Its door was blocked by huge stones,
and when these had been removed, three granite portcullises, in close succession, guarded the vault beyond.
In this apartment, which measures forty-six feet by
twelve, and is nearly under the apex of the pyramid,
a sarcophagus had apparently been sunk, but none
remained. The floor was covered with its fragments
(as Perring supposed) in red granite ; and Bunsen ascribes
the fracture to Egyptian violence. Others, however,
imagine these fragments to be only the chippings made
by the masons in fitting the portcullises.

Beyond and below this vault is a second, somewhat

---

[1] " The pyramid of Menkaura at Gizeh is far smaller than those
of his predecessors ; and it is also far inferior in accuracy. But the
masonry is good, and it is built in a more costly manner."—Petrie,
History of Egypt, vol. i. p. 72.

D

smaller, in which General Vyse found an elegant sarcophagus of basalt : " the outside was very beautifully
carved in compartments in the Doric style," or rather,
" had the deep cornice which is characteristic of the
Egyptian style." It was empty, and the lid was found
broken in the larger apartment. This valuable relic
being very brittle, and in danger of disappearing under
the curiosity of visitors, General Vyse removed the
sarcophagus with great difficulty, and embarked it for
England in 1838, but the vessel which conveyed it unfortunately went down off the coast of Spain.

The Red Pyramid was opened by the Moslems in
the thirteenth century, when, the narrator states, " nothing
was found but the decayed rotten remains of
a man, but there were no treasures, excepting
some golden tablets, inscribed with characters
which nobody could understand." Some
portion of the remains were found in the
outer apartment, which are now deposited in
the British Museum. Amongst them was the
lid of a sarcophagus inscribed with an epitaph
containing the king's name, which is at once identified
with Mycerinus, to whom Herodotus attributes the
erection of the pyramid.

Cartouche of Mycerinus.

At the eastern edge of the platform at Gîzeh
stands the Great Sphinx, a fabulous monster, com-
pounded of the bust of a man with the body and legs of
a lion. This combination is supposed to symbolise the
union of intellect and power required in a king. The
conception originated apparently in Thebes, and seems
as intimately connected with that city as the pyramid is
with Memphis. This gigantic monster is consequently
some centuries later than the neighbouring Pyramids.

Bunsen is inclined to assign it to Thothmes IV., who is represented, in a tablet on the breast of the Sphinx, offering incense and libations.[1]

It is carved out of the living rock, excavated for the purpose to a depth of about sixty feet. The sands had so accumulated about the figure, that only the head, neck, and top of the back were visible, when Caviglia began to excavate the front in 1817. In recent years it has been wholly uncovered by M. Mariette. The figure lies with its face to the Nile, with the paws protruding, in an attitude of majestic repose. The countenance has the semi-negro, or ancient Egyptian cast of features, but is much injured by the Arabs hurling their spears and arrows at the " idol." Fragments of the beard have been found, and some traces of red remain on the cheeks, which are perhaps of a later date. The head was covered with a cap, of which only the lower part remains. It is named in the hieroglyphics *Hor-em-Khoo*, " Horus in the horizon ; " that is to say, the Sun-god, the type of all the kings.

The height from the crown of the head to the floor between the paws is seventy feet ; the body is a hundred and forty feet in length, and the paws protrude fifty feet more. Between them was the altar or temple where sacrifices were offered to the deity, which was apparently the Genius of the Theban monarchy. Ramses the

---

[1] There is no foundation for the idea that the Sphinx dates from several centuries later than the Pyramids. The inscription of Thothmes IV., referred to in the text, proves, as a matter of fact, that the Sphinx was already ancient and the reverence attaching to it diminished by lapse of time at the date of this king's reign ; for it describes how, when he had fallen asleep in the shadow of the great statue, the God Ra Harmakhis appeared to him and commanded him to clear his image from the sand which was drifting over it— which the king in due course did.

Great is among the worshippers, and inscriptions on the paws testify to the continuance of the rite in the Roman age.   A small building on the steps in front is inscribed to the Emperor Severus, who visited Egypt A.D. 202.

From the floor, where the altar stood, a flight of forty-three steps ascended to a platform, whence an inclined plane led to the top of the rock facing the Sphinx.   The whole intermediate space had been excavated with prodigious labour.   Nothing could be grander than the appearance of this mysterious creature fronting the worshippers, and rising more and more over their heads, as they descended the long flight of steps to lay their offerings at its feet.

The platform of Gîzeh abounds in tombs of various ages, and more than a hundred have been opened by Lepsius.   One adorned with pillars, and brilliantly painted, was the resting-place of a " Prince Merhet," a priest, and, as Lepsius thinks, " more than probable," a son of Chufu ; he is described as " superintendent of the royal buildings."   From these tombs the enthusiastic explorer says—" I could almost write a court and state directory of the time of King Cheops or Chephren." [1] In another row of tombs Lepsius imagines he has discovered the remains of the Fifth Dynasty, hitherto supposed to have reigned at Elephantine contemporaneously with the Fourth at Memphis ; but we must certainly hesitate to accept his conclusions, when he tells us, " these are formed into one civilised epoch, dating about the year 4000 B.C.[1]   The common fault of Egyptologists is to assume a chronology in their own minds, and then attach it to the monuments, as if it were inscribed on them in unmistakable characters.   Lepsius acknowledges

[1] *Letters*, iv.

that he has " not found a single cartouche that can be safely assigned to a period previous to the Fourth Dynasty. The builders of the Great Pyramid seem to assert their right to form the commencement of monumental history." The date of his " civilised epoch," therefore, will depend on that of the Pyramids, which no sober chronology places higher than 2400 B.C., while much may be said for a later date.[1]

The ascent of the Great Pyramid is a rather laborious task. The great blocks of stone form a series of steps of unequal height, varying from two to four or five feet. A tribe of Arabs occupying a village at the foot claim the right to assist travellers. Their sheikh levies a tribute of two shillings upon each person making the ascent, and appoints two or three of his people to help him up. The difficulty is thus materially diminished, and the magnificent view from the summit—even finer, in some respects, than that from the Citadel—amply repays the traveller for the toil he has undergone. The desert stretches to the verge of the horizon. A narrow valley, inclosed by the Libyan and the Mokattam Mountains, runs to the southward. In the centre of this valley the noble river is seen winding along, with a belt of verdure on either side. The emerald green of the cultivated soil contrasts finely with the red of the mountains and the tawny sand of the desert. The pyramids of Sakkâra, the palm groves of Mitrahineh, Cairo, with its innumerable minarets and cupolas, and the Citadel seated

---

[1] On the short Berlin system of Egyptian dating, the date of the Great Pyramid would be about 3100 B.C., on Petrie's system it would be about 4685 B.C. The Berlin dating represents absolutely the lowest limit which can be assigned to the Pyramid, and even so it is 700 years older than the date assigned to it in the text, while if Petrie's date is accepted the date of the text is too modest by over 2200 years !

on its rocky height above the city, make up a picture which can scarcely be equalled, and which once seen can never be forgotten.

It is difficult, however, to abandon oneself to the full enjoyment of the scene. Crowds of Arabs follow the party to the summit, and pester them with entreaties for backsheesh, or with clamorous recommendations of the forged antiquities they have for sale. They are merry, good-humoured fellows, quick at taking a joke, and, great as the annoyance may be, it is impossible to lose one's temper. I tried the effect of a retort upon them by asking backsheesh in return. One ragged scoundrel drew himself up with a dignified air, and putting his hand into some mysterious pocket of a cotton shirt, the only garment he possessed, drew out a small coin worth about half a farthing. Putting it into my hand with a condescending gesture, he folded his arms and walked away, amidst shouts of laughter from his comrades. To one of the dealers in forged antiquities, I said, " I shan't buy those ; they were made in Birmingham." A rival trader plucked me by the coat, and said, " No, Mr. Doctor, his were not made in Birmingham ; his were made in London ; " and then proceeded to vouch for his own as " *bono anticos.*" One great feat is for an Arab to leap down the side of the First Pyramid, run across the intervening space of desert sand, and up the Second Pyramid in nine minutes. The sheikh was demanding a shilling apiece from the twenty-four Europeans who were on the summit. I remonstrated, saying that a dollar for the whole was the regular tariff. The sheikh drew me aside and whispered in my ear, " Mr. Doctor, you say nothing, and pay nothing." When he came round to collect the money from the contributors, he passed me by with a merry wink and shrug of his shoulders. A member of our party had a very powerful opera-glass, which he lent to one of the Arabs. Mohammed, looking through it, was beyond measure astounded to see not only his village in the plain below, but his two wives, Fatima and Zuleika, gaily disporting themselves in his absence, little thinking that " he held them with his glittering eye." When he had given free vent to his feelings, I said to him, " Mohammed, how do you keep two wives in order? We in England find one quite as much as we can manage with advantage; sometimes rather more." He replied, " Oh, Mr. Doctor, dey berry good; dey like two sisters; I give them much stick; " and I have no doubt that they had a good deal of stick on his return home.

All this may seem quite out of keeping with the feelings proper to a visit to the Pyramids—as no doubt it is—but I have been so much annoyed by the unreality and sentimentalism of many books of travel, that I prefer to state facts exactly as they happened. The gift of a shilling to the sheikh, on condition that he allowed no one to speak to me for a quarter of an hour, at length secured a brief interval of quiet, in which I abandoned myself to the undisturbed enjoyment of the scene and its associations. What a wonderful history is unrolled before us as we look around! Across that waste of sand, which stretches away to the north-east, came Abram and Sarai his wife, and his nephew Lot, " to sojourn in the land." The young Hebrew slave, who should rise to be second only to Pharaoh, is brought by the same route, and is followed once and again by his brethren seeking corn in Egypt. Where the palm-trees cluster so thickly round the ruined mounds on the banks of the river, Moses and

Aaron stood before the king, and demanded that he should let the people go.[1]   It was across the plain at our feet that the armies of Shishak and Pharaoh Necho marched for the invasion of Palestine.   Here, too, came the fugitives, Jeroboam, Urijah, and others,[2] seeking refuge amongst their ancestral enemies.   Near that obelisk of red granite rising amid the glossy green of the sugar-canes, Joseph married his wife : and when the Jewish monarchy had fallen, Onias, the high-priest, erected a temple upon the plan of that at Jerusalem for his brethren who had settled in Egypt.   There, too, if we may trust tradition, the infant Saviour was brought when escaping from the wrath of " Herod the king."   Turning from sacred to secular history, memories of Persian, Macedonian, and Roman conquerors—Cambyses, Alexander, and Cæsar —start into life as we look down upon the plain.   Again the scene changes, as Amrou and Omar unfurl the banner of the False Prophet, and wrest the richest province of the empire from the enfeebled hand of the Byzantine rulers.   Again, as we gaze, we seem to see at the head of his armies the magnificent Emir Yusef Salah-e'deen march from Cairo to confront the Crusaders under Richard the Lion-hearted, King of England, and, having given some of its most romantic chapters to modern

[1] It is somewhat unlikely that the scene of the interviews of Moses and Aaron with the Pharaoh of the Exodus was anywhere near Memphis. The capital, in the XVIIIth Dynasty, was at Thebes, while in the XIXth Dynasty the royal residence was sometimes at Thebes, and sometimes at the new Delta capital, Pi-Ramessu, which has been identified with Pelusium.   " It is clear," says Professor Peet (Egypt and the Old Testament, pp. 85, 86), " from Ex. xii. 47, and Num. xxxiii. 3–6, that it was at Rameses that Moses stood before Pharaoh, and from Rameses that the Exodus began."   In any case Memphis can scarcely lay claim to the distinction of having been the scene of the birth of the Israelite nation.

[2] 1 Kings xi. 40 ; xiv. 25, 26 ; Jeremiah xxvi. 21 ; xli. 17 ; xliii. 7.

history, to return, and dying, send his shroud round the city, whilst criers went before it exclaiming, " This is all that remains of the pomp of Saladin." Coming down to our own times, we cannot forget the Battle of the Pyramids when a small compact French army withstood the attack of 60,000 Mamelukes and compelled them to retreat, leaving 15,000 dead upon the field. In the four thousand years over which the history of Egypt extends, what generations have lived and died, what empires have risen and flourished and decayed ! Surrounded by these affecting memorials of bygone ages, we seem to hear a voice sounding from the silence of the past, and saying, " All flesh is grass, and all the goodliness thereof is as the flower of the field : the grass withereth, the flower fadeth : . . . but the word of our God shall stand for ever." [1]

[1] Isaiah xl. 6, 8.

CHAPTER II

CAIRO TO ASSOUAN

"CAIRO to Assiût direct by railway!" Grotesque as this sounds, it has for some years been possible, a railway having been constructed over the 230 miles separating the two towns. Few persons, however, would care to " do " the Nile in this fashion.[1]

The traveller, who wishes really to enjoy the journey, has the choice of two preferable modes of transit. He may go by steamer or by dahabiyeh. If pressed for time and of limited purse, he must needs choose the former. If he is able to control abundant supply of money and time he may choose the latter. Since 1870 the steamer arrangements on the Nile have been passing more and more completely under the control of Messrs. T. Cook & Son. This firm has now almost a monopoly of the steamer traffic on the Nile. The result is that a regular service of boats runs between Cairo and the First Cataract twice weekly during the season, from November to March. New steamers, constructed with a knowledge of all the special requirements of the service, have begun running this year (1886); and what used to be both a

[1] These and other references to modes of travel date, of course, from the '70's of the nineteenth century, when the organisation of Egyptian travel was in its infancy.

formidable and costly journey, is now within the reach of all who can afford to visit the East. Travellers who make the journey by dahabiyeh often find that the smoothness and enjoyment of the trips are increased by leaving the needful arrangements in the hands of the same firm.

The chief advantage of the steamboat trip is that we are able to run rapidly past the uninteresting portions of the river. The Nile scenery is for the most part dull and flat. On a dahabiyeh we may find ourselves becalmed for days off a mud-bank or a long stretch of sand, with nothing to do except watching the antics or listening to the monotonous singing of the crew. If, weary of waiting for a wind, the crew are ordered to tow the boat against the stream, the progress is exceedingly slow and tedious —six or eight miles a day are the utmost that can be accomplished.

But steamboat speed is not secured without great compensating disadvantages. The delicious sense of repose, the Oriental *Kièf*, the Italian *dolce far niente*, which constitutes so large a part of the enjoyment of the Nile trip, is impossible on board a steamer. Though the rate of progress be slow as compared with that on European or American waters, it is yet far too rapid to let us abandon ourselves to the lotus-eating indolence which is so refreshing to the wearied frame and over-wrought brain of the traveller in search of health. Then, too, it is impossible to linger where we please. We must hurry on. Two hours may be enough for the tombs of Beni Hassan, three hours for the temple of Esneh, four days for Luxor and Karnak ; but it is distressing to feel that we cannot stop if we like. Haunted by the fear of being too late, we complete our survey, watch

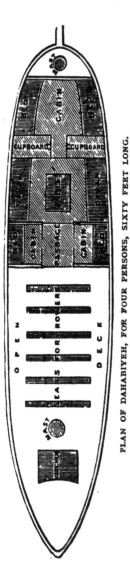

PLAN OF DAHABIYEH, FOR FOUR PERSONS, SIXTY FEET LONG.

in hand, to be sure of catching the steamer before she leaves her moorings in the river. The risk of finding uncongenial company on board is likewise not inconsiderable. In a public conveyance it is not possible to choose one's fellow-travellers, and it may happen that our meditations on the grand memories of the past are being perpetually broken in upon by " men whose talk is of bullocks." A very serious objection to the old steamers used to be their scandalously dirty condition, and the swarms of vermin with which they were infested. This, of course, does not now apply ; the new vessels being as clean and as comfortable as the most fastidious can desire. Nevertheless, for those who have ample means and leisure, and who have resources within themselves, or in their party, to bear the monotony of some days or weeks on board a boat with nothing to do and little to see, the Nile trip in a dahabiyeh is one of the most delightful excursions in the world.[1]   To others the steamer offers a very fair substitute.

But what is a dahabiyeh ? The dahabiyeh, gentle reader, is a boat in form and outline not unlike the barges of the City Companies in the days when the Thames was to Londoners what the Nile is to the Egyptians. Its saloons and cabins are on deck. Some are luxuriously fitted up, room being found even for a piano. They differ in size, affording accommodation for from two to six or eight passengers. For the crew no sleeping accommodation whatever is provided. They roll themselves up in their *burnouses* and lie down on the foredeck like bundles of old clothes, for which I have not infrequently mistaken them. The boat is worked by two large triangular sails fitted to masts fore and aft, and there are benches for rowers when needed. The resemblance between the Nile boats of the present day and those of the ancient Egyptians, as depicted on the monuments, has been often noticed. " Joseph, in the flush of power, probably journeyed thus through Egypt, only, of course, with a royal magnificence and splendour of appointment to be dreamed of rather than described. All the travel of those days between the upper and lower country, the traffic of Thebes and Memphis, would be done in such vessels. It must be remembered, that, although Egypt is nearly eight hundred miles in length, its average breadth is only ten or twelve, of which the river is the great feature, the centre and source of fertility and wealth. Thus every city was by the water side. Egypt was emphatically " a place of broad rivers

---

[1] As a representation of the spirit of Nile travel in a dahabiyeh, nothing can be better than the picture drawn by Miss Amelia Edwards in *A Thousand Miles up the Nile*.

and streams," white, in those palmy days, with the swelling sail of many a gallant ship, and populous with galleys. So conservative, too, in its customs was it, that even the Ptolemies and Romans were forced to follow them. Thus perhaps Cleopatra's famous barge may have been but a gorgeous dahabiyeh :—

> " The barge she sat in, like a burnished throne,
> Burned on the water, the poop was beaten gold.
> Purple the sails, and so perfumèd that
> The winds were love-sick with them : the oars were silver,
> Which to the tune of flutes kept stroke."

Dahabiyehs run up the river without stopping, except when becalmed or to lie-to for the night. Places of interest are visited on the return to Cairo. It will, however, suit our convenience better to take them in reverse order.

Our first halting-place will be Bedresheyn, fifteen miles from Bûlâk, to visit the site of ancient Memphis and the Pyramids of Sakkâra. There is a curious Mussulman tradition in connection with this village, from which its name is said to have been derived. The orthodox creed of Islam is that women will be saved like men, and will be made young again on entering heaven. This legend, however, affirms that there is one exception to the rule. Joseph, when Grand Vizier of Egypt, was riding out from Memphis, when an aged woman accosted him and implored alms. So wrinkled and deformed was she, that he could not help exclaiming, " How ugly thou art ! " " Pray, then, to Allah," she replied, " that he would make me young and beautiful. He hears all thy prayers, and grants whatever thou dost ask." Thereupon Joseph lifted up his hands and prayed for her as she requested. Instantly she stood by his side transformed into a lovely girl—so lovely that he was enamoured of her and made her his wife. She lived long, and survived him for many years. Dying in extreme old age, she went to heaven, an old woman, the only old woman there : for Allah makes all good women young again once, but once only, and she can never be made young again.

The road from the village leads through one of the most luxuriant palm forests to be found in Egypt. Our boat was moored for the night close to the point where an avenue of trees came down to the river-bank. The full moon was shining with wonderful brilliancy, pouring a flood of light over the landscape, of which we, in these northern latitudes, can form little conception. I went ashore and wandered for hours among the tall columnar stems and under the graceful feathery crowns of the palm-trees. A party of villagers, too astonished even to ask for backsheesh, came out to gaze at the strange sight of a European wandering about after nightfall. On my expressing a wish for some of the fronds which hung overhead, a lithe, agile fellow clambered up like a monkey and plucked half a dozen for me. Among the many pleasant memories which I brought back from Egypt there are none more pleasant than that of the moonlight walk through the palm groves of Mitrahineh.

There are few remains above ground of the splendour of ancient Memphis. The city has utterly disappeared. If any traces of it yet exist, they are buried beneath the vast mounds of crumbling bricks and broken pottery which meet the eye in every direction. Near the village of Mitrahineh is a colossal statue of Ramses the Great. It is apparently one of two described by Herodotus and Diodorus as standing in front of the

Temple of Ptah. They were originally about fifty feet in height. The one which remains, though mutilated, measures forty-eight feet. It is finely carved in a limestone which takes a high polish, and is evidently a portrait. It lies in a pit, which during the inundation is filled with water.[1]   As we gaze at this fallen and battered statue of the mighty conqueror, who was probably contemporaneous with Moses, it is impossible not to remember the words of the prophet Isaiah :—" They that see thee shall narrowly look upon thee, and consider thee, saying, Is this the man that made the earth to tremble, that did shake kingdoms ; that made the world as a wilderness, and destroyed the cities thereof ; that opened not the house of his prisoners ? All the kings of the nations, even all of them, lie in glory, every one in his own house. But thou art cast out of thy grave like an abominable branch, and as the raiment of those that are slain, thrust through with a sword, that go down to the stones of the pit." [2]

Riding across the mounds of débris already referred to, we soon reach the vast subterranean tomb in which, for a period of at least fifteen hundred years, the bodies of the sacred bulls were interred. In the year 1851, M. Mariette observed the head of a sphinx protruding from the sand, and remembered that Strabo described the Serapeum of Memphis as approached through an avenue of sphinxes. He at once commenced his explorations in search of the temple in which Apis was worshipped when alive, and the tomb in which it was buried when dead. With immense exertions, the sand-drift was

[1] The colossal statue of Ramses II. has now been raised above the inundation level, and put under cover. It was discovered by Caviglia and Sloane in 1820, and its original height was 42 feet.
[2] Isaiah xiv. 16–19

SARCOPHAGUS IN THE SERAPEUM OF MEMPHIS.

cleared away, and the avenue was laid bare from beneath
a superincumbent mass, which was in some places
seventy feet in depth.   The splendour of this imposing
approach may be inferred from the fact that one hundred
and forty-one sphinxes were discovered *in situ*, besides
the pedestals of many others.   The temple to which
they led has disappeared, but the tomb remains.   It
consists of a huge vault or tunnel, divided into three
parts, one of which was four hundred yards in length,
another two hundred and ten yards.   Only the latter
of these is now accessible.   Chambers lead out from it
on either side, in each of which is a ponderous granite
sarcophagus hollowed out in the centre.   In this cavity,
which will hold four or five persons with ease, the
embalmed body of the sacred bull was deposited.   A
granite slab of great size and weight, placed over the
sarcophagus, closed it like a lid.   The Khedive, anxious
to place one of these sarcophagi in his museum at Bûlâk,
succeeded in conveying it from the chamber into the
subterranean passage.   But there it remains.   The
inclined plane which leads to the surface of the soil
offers an insurmountable obstacle to its further progress.[1]
Yet the ancient Egyptians transported these huge blocks
of granite from the quarries near Syene to Memphis, a
distance of nearly six hundred miles !

The pomp and splendour with which the worship of
the bull Apis was celebrated at Memphis may help us
to understand the apostasy of the Israelites in the wilderness, when, having made a molten calf, they said, " These
be thy gods, O Israel, which brought thee up out of the

---

[1] " The lid and the sarcophagus, which belong to one another, were
probably stopped here on their way to the vault for which they were
destined, in consequence of the overthrow of the worship of Apis."
—Baedeker, *Egypt*.

land of Egypt." [1]   They had been so accustomed to see divine honours paid, even by the mightiest of their task-masters, to this supposed incarnation of the Deity, that at Sinai itself they yielded to the influence of long habit, and " corrupted themselves, turning aside quickly out of the way which the Lord commanded them."

It was not the bull alone which was worshipped during life by the Egyptians and embalmed on its death.   Every nome, almost every city, had its tutelar animal, which received similar honours.   Dogs, cats, jackals, wolves, crocodiles, baboons, held in abhorrence in one district, were revered in another.   Thus the Tentyrites, regarding the crocodile as the symbol of Typhon, killed it as a religious duty.   Elsewhere, temples were built in its honour, in which these disgusting reptiles were tended with the most sedulous care.   In all parts of Egypt are large pits, in which the embalmed remains of various animals are to be found in prodigious numbers.   One species of ibis seems to have been worshipped everywhere. The bird itself has disappeared, but its embalmed remains exist by millions.   Bayle St. John, who made his way into the Ibis pits near Memphis, says : " We began to explore a vast succession of galleries and apartments, closed up here and there with walls of unburnt brick. I can give no idea of the extent of these bird catacombs, except by saying that they appeared large enough to contain all the defunct members of the feathered creation since the beginning of the world.   Some of the chambers were vast caves, and there were hundreds of them."   It was scarcely an exaggeration of the Roman satirist, who, when ridiculing the animal worship of the Egyptians,

[1] Exodus xxxii. 4, 8.

said that it was " more easy in Egypt to find a god than a man."

In the sandy plains near the site of Memphis are the Pyramids of Sakkâra. They stand in a vast necropolis four and a half miles in length, where lie interred the dead of the earliest periods of Egyptian history. One of them is built in stages, and is said, by a doubtful tradition preserved by Manetho, to have been erected by a monarch of the First Dynasty. If this be true, it is much older than those of Gîzeh, and is the most ancient monument in the world.[1] The Gîzeh Pyramids, from their superior size and imposing position, have come to be spoken of as *the Pyramids*, leading many persons to suppose that they are the only ones. This, however, is a mistake. There are eleven still standing in Sakkâra. Throwing out of account various pyramidal structures in Upper Egypt, Ethiopia, and elsewhere, the total number may be put down at about a hundred. They are not scattered indiscriminately throughout the country but occupy an area about forty-five miles in length, from Gîzeh in the north to the Fâyûm in the south. Some persons have conjectured that their concentration within these limits seems to point to some peculiar phase of religion or civilisation as prevailing at the period of their erection, and that they were built, not by a native Egyptian race, but by foreign conquerors, who had placed their capital at Memphis, and introduced this mode of sepulchre, which lasted only during their period of

[1] The Step-Pyramid of Saqqara was erected for King Zeser of the IIIrd Dynasty by his famous architect, Imhotep, who was afterwards deified, and under the Greek form of his name, Imouthis, was identified with Asklepios or Æsculapius. Zeser's Pyramid is the oldest large stone building in the world, and is only antedated by the small stone chamber of the tomb of Khasekhemui of the IInd Dynasty at Abydos.

occupation, and ceased when they were expelled. This view has not found favour with Egyptologists, and there can be no doubt that they were pyramid-sepulchres.

We cannot leave the plain of Memphis without recurring yet once again to the most memorable event in all its eventful history. It was probably here that Moses and Aaron stood before Pharaoh and demanded that he should let the people go. In the city now buried beneath mouldering heaps and desert sand the faithful and fearless leader braved the " wrath of the king : for he endured, as seeing Him who is invisible." This was the spot where " Pharaoh rose up in the night, he, and all his servants, and all the Egyptians ; and there was a great cry in Egypt ; for there was not a house where there was not one dead." [1]   Our thoughts pass away from the palaces smitten with this sudden and sore bereavement to the homes of the enslaved race waiting securely for the signal to depart, whilst through faith they " kept the passover, and the sprinkling of blood, lest He that destroyed the first-born should touch them." [2] Great as was the historical importance of this event, seeing that it was the birth of a nation, it gains yet deeper significance in the fact that it was a type of the great Antitype : " For even Christ our passover is sacrificed for us." [3]

It is of the next one hundred and fifty or two hundred miles of the journey up the Nile that travellers often complain as being tedious and wearisome. The scenery is monotonous, and the monumental remains are few and unimportant. And yet I cannot say that I felt

---

[1] See note to p. 56.   [2] Hebrews xi. 28.
[3] 1 Corinthians v. 7.

either tedium or weariness. The great river itself is
a constant source of wonder. For fifteen hundred miles
below the point at which the Tacazze enters it from the
mountains of Abyssinia, it flows onward to the sea without receiving a single tributary. Not even a tiny rill
or brooklet trickles through the desert sand throughout
this immense distance, and rain is almost unknown. The
main occupation of the peasantry on its banks is to pump
water from its ample stream. Sâkiyehs and shâdûfs
are busy all day and all night long levying contributions
upon it for the irrigation of the land. Absorbed throughout its course by the scorching sand, and evaporated by
an unclouded sun, its volume remains apparently un-
diminished. Fed by the lakes, and annually swollen
by the tropical rains of Central Africa, it is an object of
ceaseless interest.

Then the atmospheric phenomena are of great variety
and beauty. There is, indeed, no " weather " on the
Nile, in our English sense of the term. By force of
habit we commence the voyage by saying, " Fine morning ; " " Fine evening ; " but gradually we awake to
the consciousness that every day is fine. The subtle
criticisms, the striking and original remarks on the
weather, which make up so large a part of the small talk
of conversation at home, are felt to be absurdly out of
place where rain is almost a prodigy. In the early spring
the *khamsîn* does, indeed, afford a very unpleasant change
to comment upon. It is a hot, dry wind, laden with
fine particles of dust, which penetrate everywhere, fill
one's eyes and ears, irritate the skin, and produce a sense
of extreme discomfort. Everything is seen through a
lurid haze. The sands of the desert are whirled by it
into rotating columns, which march to and fro till they

suddenly break up and disappear. On the river this is merely a cause of annoyance, but in the desert it becomes a serious danger. Caravans are said to have perished and been buried beneath the drifting sands. Apart from this most undesirable " change in the weather," the days resemble one another. But the parts of each day have to the observant eye an ever-varying charm. The mornings are delightful, clear and cool and bright, with no mist to blur the outlines or veil the sun. Towards mid-day, all colour seems to be discharged from the landscape, which is wrapped in a white, blinding glare. Yet even now it is pleasant to lie under an awning on deck, and with a feeling of delicious indolence listen to the lapping of the water against the sides of the boat, and watch the banks glide past us as in a dream. With the drawing on of evening a glory of colour comes out in the light of the setting sun. Purple shadows are cast by the mountains. The reds and greys of sandstone, granite, and limestone cliffs blend exquisitely with the tawny yellow of the desert, the rich green of the banks, and the blue of the river, giving combinations and contrast of colour in which the artist revels. The cold grey twilight follows immediately upon sunset ; but in a few minutes there is a marvellous change. The earth and sky are suffused with a delicate pink tinge, known as the after-glow. This is the most fairy-like and magical effect of colour I have ever seen. Swiss travellers are familiar with something like it in the rosy flush of the snowy Alps before sunrise and after sunset. The peculiarity in Egypt is that light and colour return after an interval of ashy grey, like the coming back of life to a corpse, and that it is not confined to a part of the landscape, but floods the whole. I have seen no

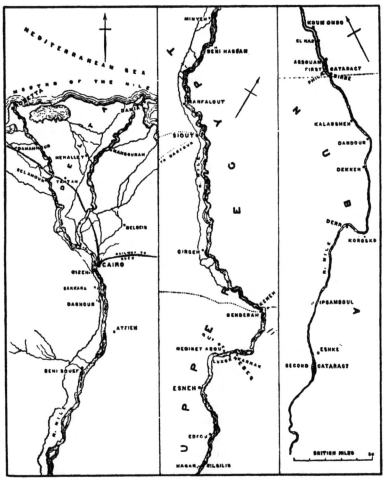

THE NILE, FROM ROSETTA TO THE SECOND CATARACT.

explanation of this most beautiful phenomenon, and can only conjecture that it is connected with the reflection and refraction of the light of the setting sun from the sands of the Libyan Desert. Then comes on the night —and such a night! The stars shine with a lustrous brilliancy so intense that I have seen a distinct shadow cast by the planet Jupiter, whilst his satellites were easily visible through an ordinary opera-glass.[1] Orion was an object of indescribable splendour. Under which of her aspects the moon was most beautiful I cannot say —whether the first slender thread of light, invisible in our denser atmosphere, or in her growing brightness, or in her full-orbed radiance. Addison's familiar lines gained a new meaning when read under this hemisphere of glory :

> " Soon as the evening shades prevail,
> The moon takes up the wondrous tale,
> And, nightly, to the listening earth,
> Repeats the story of her birth ;
> Whilst all the stars that round her burn,
> And all the planets in their turn,
> Confirm the tidings as they roll,
> And spread the truth from pole to pole."

The river flows on through a narrow strip of vegetation varying from a few feet to a few miles in width, but always bounded by the desert. Sometimes the mountains retreat to a considerable distance from the river, sometimes they come down to its very brink, and form a series of bold cliffs, often surmounted by a Coptic convent. The villages are commonly picturesque, as seen from a distance, standing as they do under a grove

[1] On one occasion we believed that we could see the principal satellite with the naked eye. Is this possible ? (Dr. Manning's question may be answered in the affirmative. Such observations have been made, not often, but by such skilful observers as Jacob, Heis, Webb, Denning, and Todd. See Webb's *Celestial Objects*.)

of palms, and often placed on the top of a mound which hides the ruins of an ancient city. But on a nearer approach they are dirty and dilapidated beyond description. Still these wretched squalid hamlets have a charm for the European traveller. The minaret of the mosque, though often constructed only of mud, is brilliant with white-wash, and it rises gracefully amongst the palm-trees. At sunset, after nightfall, at daybreak, at noon, and towards evening, the Muezzin takes his stand in the gallery, and in a loud, sonorous voice calls the faithful to prayer—" God is most great. I testify that there is no Deity but God. I testify that Mohammed is God's apostle. Come to prayer. Come to security. God is most great ; " adding, during the night, and in the early morning, " Prayer is better than sleep." Attached to the mosque is commonly a school, the noise of which is a sufficient guide to the spot. The children recite their lessons all together, and each scholar endeavours to make his voice heard above the din by shouting his loudest. The instruction given is of the slightest possible kind, consisting of little else than the recitation of the Korán and the simplest rules of arithmetic. The master is often a blind man, who, being able to repeat the Korán by rote, can teach it to the children. His payment is little more than nominal, but is apparently quite equal to his merits. Mr. Lane gives some curious illustrations of the nature of the instruction given, and tells the following droll story : " I was lately told of a man who could neither read nor write succeeding to the office of a schoolmaster in my neighbourhood. Being able to recite the whole of the Korán, he could hear the boys repeat their lessons : to write them, he employed the ' 'areef ' (or head_boy and monitor in the school), pretending that his eyes were weak. A few days after he had taken upon himself this office, a poor woman brought a letter for him to read to her from her son, who had gone on pilgrimage. The fikee pretended to read it, but said nothing ; and the woman, inferring from his silence that the letter contained bad news, said to him :—' Shall I shriek ? ' He answered ' Yes.' ' Shall I tear my clothes ? ' she asked. He replied, ' Yes.' So the poor woman returned to her house, and with her assembled friends performed the lamentation and other ceremonies usual on the occasion of a death. Not many days after this, her son arrived, and she asked him what he could mean by causing a letter to be written stating that he was dead. He explained the contents of the letter, and she went to the schoolmaster and begged him to inform her why he had told her to shriek, and to tear her clothes, since the letter was to inform her that her son was well, and he was now arrived at home. Not at all abashed, he said, ' God knows futurity. How could I know that your son would arrive in safety ? It was better that you should think him dead than be led to expect to see him, and perhaps be disappointed.' Some persons who were sitting with him praised his wisdom, exclaiming, ' Truly our new fikee is a man of unusual judgment,' and for a little while he found that he had raised his reputation by this blunder."

The profusion of bird life on the Nile is one of its most striking features. Myriads of storks, cranes, geese, wild ducks, pelicans, hawks, pigeons, and herons are seen clustering on the islands in the river, lining its banks, or flying in dense clouds overhead. To protect the growing crops the fellaheen often construct little stands for boys armed with slings, who acquire wonderful dexterity in bringing down their feathered game. In Ancient Egypt birds were as numerous as now. Geese are represented as forming an important part of every banquet, and they are seldom wanting in the offerings to the gods. Fowling was a favourite amusement.

EGYPTIAN FOWLER.
(From the British Museum.)

Visitors to the British Museum are familiar with the tablet which represents the flocks of geese possessed by a large landed proprietor. In another the sportsman is seen catching water-fowl in a thicket of papyrus and lotus-lilies on the river-bank; a decoy duck stands on the prow of his boat, and a cat is trained to act as a retriever. These countless flocks of birds may serve to illustrate the dream of Pharaoh's chief baker. " I had three white baskets on my head : and in the uppermost basket there was of all manner of bakemeats for Pharaoh ; and the birds did eat them out of the basket upon my head." [1]

Quadrupeds are much less numerous. As in all Oriental countries, homeless, masterless dogs roam round the villages, and act as scavengers. Among the swamps of the Delta wild boars are common. Jackals and foxes may be met with everywhere. In the neighbourhood of Luxor and Karnak a hyæna is often seen, with its heavy, clumsy form and slouching gait, prowling amongst the ruins. The crocodile has almost disappeared from Lower Egypt. Notwithstanding its impenetrable coat of mail and its terrible jaws, it is a shy, timid creature, and is said to have been driven away by the paddle-wheels of the steamboats. Formerly they might occasionally be seen sunning themselves on the mud and sandbanks between Keneh and Assouan, but they have not been seen between these points now for a number of years past. It is only as we enter Nubia that they are found in considerable numbers.

The flora of Egypt is not very remarkable. Excepting palms, the trees are few and unimportant. A few fine sycamores may be seen, generally in the neighbourhood of a mosque, or shadowing a *santon's* tomb. Midway between Cairo and the First Cataract the doumpalm makes its appearance. It differs greatly from the ordinary date-palm. Instead of the single straight stem, it divides into two main branches, which again bifurcate as the tree grows. Its fruit, which is about the size and colour of a pomegranate, is said to taste like gingerbread. It contains an exceedingly hard stone, which is used by

[1] Genesis xl. 16, 17.

the modern, as it was by the ancient, Egyptian carpenters for making sockets, drills, and hinges.

One very remarkable change has passed upon the water-plants of the Nile. The lotus and the papyrus were formerly the most common and characteristic of

EGYPTIAN ENTERTAINMENT; EACH GUEST WITH A LOTUS FLOWER.
(From the British Museum.)

its products, insomuch that they formed the symbols of Upper and Lower Egypt. The papyrus was used not only for making paper, to which it gave its name, but for the construction of boats, baskets, and innumerable other articles; as in the Upper Jordan Valley, where it still grows abundantly, even cottages were built with it. No religious service, no state ceremonial, no domestic festival is found without the lotus flower. It forms part of every offering to the gods. The guests at a banquet all hold one in their hands. It is, perhaps, the object of all others most constantly represented on the monuments. Yet both the lotus and the papyrus have disappeared from Egypt. No trace of either can be found.[1] Unaccountable as is the disappearance of these plants, it was yet foretold by the prophet Isaiah, as a part of the Divine judgment upon Egypt: " The brooks of defence shall be emptied and dried up : the reeds and flags shall wither. The paper reeds by the brooks . . . and everything sown by the brooks, shall wither, be driven away, and be no more." [2] The phrase " brooks of defence " in this passage has greatly perplexed commentators. Brooks, in the proper sense of the term, there are none in Egypt. Of course the reference is to the canals with which the country is intersected. But why " brooks of defence " ? It has been commonly supposed that they were constructed simply for irrigation. But it affords a striking illustration of the minute accuracy of Scripture phraseology to find that they served the further purpose of guarding the land against the raids of the Bedouin horsemen, who then, as now, infested the desert and whose depredations were checked by these canals.[3]

There is little to interest or detain us in the modern

[1] It is indeed said that, in some remote and unvisited portions of the Delta, an occasional papyrus reed may be discovered. The fact is doubted, and the statement in the text is substantially true.

[2] Isaiah xix. 6, 7.

[3] The word translated in the A. V. " of defence," really means " of Egypt," and the passage should read, " The streams (or canals) of Egypt shall be minished and dried up." See Isaiah xix. 6, R. V. and margin. There is no need for the somewhat fanciful interpretation of the text.

towns on the Nile bank. Occasionally, as at Manfalût, the governor's palace offers some characteristic bits of Arabic architecture. These, however, are rare. Even

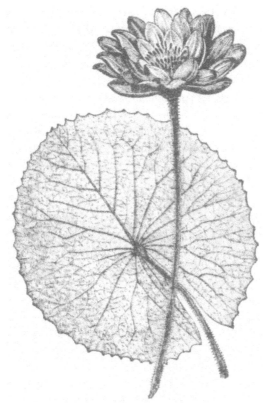

LOTUS FLOWER AND LEAF.

in the larger towns, Keneh, for instance, or Siût, there is little to be seen save wretched, dilapidated hovels, lanes almost impassable for their filth and narrowness, with, here and there, a huge sugar factory or cotton mill

worked by forced labour for the benefit of the Khedive.
The situation of Siût (Assiût, as it is now usually spelt)
is very beautiful.   A ride of about two miles over a
raised causeway, which leads amongst fields of great
fertility, brings us to a picturesque gateway not unlike
that at Manfalût.   In front of it is a large courtyard,
overshadowed by fine trees, in which are seated numbers
of fellaheen or townspeople waiting to present petitions
to the governor, or to plead their cause before him.
In one corner a group of conscripts are squatting, who
have been dragged from their homes to serve in the
army, the navy, or the factories of the Khedive, as the
officials may decide.   Entering the city gate, we find
ourselves in the capital of Upper Egypt.   The bazaars,
though dark and gloomy, are crowded with buyers and
sellers.   A military officer, peacefully mounted on a
donkey, is transacting business at the door of a money-
changer's shop.   A group of Bedouin are bargaining for
swords, daggers, and long Arab guns at an armourer's
forge.   Veiled women are haggling over the price of a
piece of blue cloth or a measure of flour.   Passing out
from this busy scene by the gate on the opposite side of
the city to that at which we entered, we find ourselves
almost immediately in the silence and solitude of the
great Libyan Desert.   Fragments of mummies, mummy-
cases, and cere-cloth lie about unheeded on the sand.
The steep, rocky hill-side is honeycombed with tombs,
in which are found remains of embalmed wolves.   It
was from the worship of these animals that the town took
its ancient name of Lycopolis.[1]   The view from the

---

[1] Assiût was in ancient days the chief seat of the worship of
Upuat or Wep-wawet, one of the gods of the dead, and the desert
wolf was sacred to him.

TEMPLE AT DENDERAH.

summit of this range of hills is very striking, especially as I saw it, at sunset. Except where the Valley of the Nile broke the monotony, the eye ranged over a boundless expanse of desert. To the very verge of the horizon stretched undulations of marl and sand, like the long swell of ocean in a calm. On the edge of the cultivated soil a few black tents of the Bedouin were pitched. Two or three Arabs, their naked bodies almost black with exposure, were stalking solemnly across the silent waste at our feet, over which long shadows were cast in the slanting beams of the setting sun. They were laden with the skins of wild beasts, which they were bringing into Siût to sell. No other living beings were visible, and they harmonised well with the sentiment of the scene. I felt at the time that the grandest mountain scenery of Switzerland was less impressive than this sublime monotony of sky and desert.

It is but seldom that ordinary travellers can have any direct communication with the people of the country. The language in most cases forms an insuperable barrier. The fellah can speak nothing but Arabic, of which the traveller is commonly quite ignorant. If the dragoman is employed as interpreter, he is pretty sure to reproduce the comical scene described by Kinglake.[1] The donkey-boys and local guides often know a little English, of which they make very droll use. I was greatly amused and puzzled by the application of the word *lunch*. " See, Osiris hab lunch," said my guide one day, pointing to an altar piled with offering before the god, sculptured on a temple wall. On another occasion, riding through some fields of *doorah* and vetch, I was told that the former was " Arabs' lunch ; " the latter, " camels' lunch."

[1] *Eothen*, vol. i. p. 12.

F

The explanation I found to be that, as Europeans break-fast and dine on board their boat, whilst lunch is often eaten on shore, it is the only meal of which the natives see or hear anything ; hence it has come to be used for food in general.

At various points along the banks of the river we may observe lines of chambers cut into the face of the cliffs. Originally tombs, they were, after the introduction of Christianity, used as cells by hermits and anchorites. The most interesting of them are at Beni Hassan, about one hundred and sixty miles above Cairo. They form a terrace, approached by the remains of an ancient causeway, which rises from the plain and runs along the front of the grottoes. The rock has been hewn out into architraves and columns, with doorways leading into the tombs. They thus have the appearance of buildings rather than caverns. The columns are remarkable for their non-Egyptian character. If found elsewhere, they would be at once classed as Doric, yet they belong to the earliest period of the Egyptian monarchy, and are probably but little later than the era of the Pyramids. No Greek influence can therefore be suspected.[1] The walls of the chambers are covered with frescoes representing the everyday life of the time. Men and women are wrestling, fishing and ploughing,

[1] The statement of the text requires a little modification. The tombs of Beni Hassan belong, not to the earliest period of the Egyptian monarchy, but to the Middle Kingdom. They are those of local governors or " nomarchs " of the XIIth Dynasty, and their date is about 1,000 years later than that of the Pyramids of Gîzeh. The " proto-Doric " columns can scarcely be said to be " non-Egyptian." On the contrary, they form one of the most notable contributions of Egypt to architecture. They occur in several other cases, notably in the famous temple of Queen Hatshepsut at Der el-Bahri, and the work of Thothmes III. at Karnak, and if there is to be any question of influence, the Egyptian column must be held to have influenced the Greek.

reaping, trapping birds, giving dinner-parties, being flogged, *cutting their toe-nails*, treading the winepress,

dancing, playing the harp, weaving linen, playing at ball, being shaved by the barber, playing at draughts. Verily, there is nothing new under the sun! Life in Egypt four thousand years ago was almost identical with that of England in the present day. One of my companions was a Cumberland squire, and a famous wrestler. His

CHRISTIAN SYMBOLS AT BENI HASSAN.

attention was riveted by a series of wall-paintings, representing athletic sports, chiefly wrestling matches. I said to him, " Are those pictures like the truth ? " He replied enthusiastically, " By Jove, there isn't a grip or a throw that I haven't used ; and I defy the best wrestler in the north of England to do it better."

In the tomb of Khnum-hetep the arrival of a party of Canaanitish shepherds in Egypt is depicted. They are being introduced to the nomarch of the district by a scribe who holds a tablet, giving their number as thirty-seven, and calling them *Amu ;* by which name the

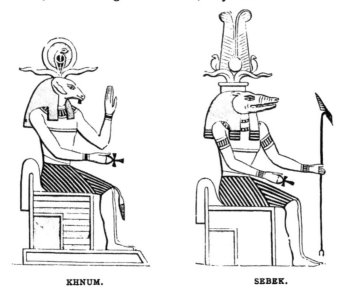

KHNUM.   SEBEK.

Aramaic races were known to the Egyptians. A hiero-glyphic inscription styles the leader of the party *Hek-absh*. He is leading a Syrian goat as a present to the nomarch, and in the panniers of the asses which follow are other presents, among them jars of stibium, at that time largely imported into Egypt from Palestine.[1] On its

---

[1] In the inscription it is said that they came from Bat Mestem, which probably means, " the stibium mine." A place of this name is mentioned in the Apocrypha as existing in the Plain of Jezreel.

VISIT OF A FAMILY OF THE SEMITIC NATION CALLED AMU TO EGYPT.

(From the Tomb of Khnum-hetep.)

first discovery this fresco was supposed to represent the coming down into Egypt of Jacob and his family. This opinion is now generally abandoned; but the fresco is interesting, as a contemporary illustration of patriarchal history.

It has been mentioned that the rock-tombs of Egypt were used after the commencement of the Christian era as the abode of monks. Of this there are many curious traces at Beni Hassan. Among the ancient frescoes, we find Christian symbols, placed there by the anchorites, and closely resembling those in the Roman catacombs. In at least two cases we have the cross upon which doves are resting, symbolising the atoning sacrifice of Christ, with the operations of the Spirit needful to give it effect upon the hearts of men. One of these has a leaf of trefoil, typical of the Trinity, and the Alpha and the Omega conjointed, so as to form a single letter. The familiar monogram of Christ into which the cross is worked is of frequent occurrence. Here, too we find the mystic *Tau*, or *crux ansata* of early Egyptian mythology, adopted as a Christian symbol. It is, at least, a wonderful coincidence—perhaps more than a coincidence —that the cross was the symbol of life among the Egyptians. The gods are constantly represented as holding it in the right hand, as shown in the engravings on page 84. We cannot wonder that the early Christians should have availed themselves of this significant fact to express their faith in Him who by the cross " abolished death, and hath brought life and immortality to light."

We have to ascend the Nile nearly three hundred and fifty miles above Cairo, one hundred and sixty above Beni Hassan, before we reach any of the great temples of Ancient Egypt. Below this point they have all been destroyed, and only their foundations can be traced. But from Girgeh up to Abû-Simbel the number and magnificence of their remains give an impressive sense

ENTRANCE TO TEMPLE, DENDERAH.

of the splendour of the kingdom of the Pharaohs. The first we reach is that of Abydos, specially dedicated to Osiris, and which contended with Philæ for the honour of being his place of burial.[1] A donkey-ride of ten or twelve miles from Girgeh across a plain of extraordinary fertility, brings us to the edge of the desert. Here are the ruins of two temples, and the mounds which cover the vast cemetery around the tomb of the deified monarch. A superstitious feeling, like that which has prevailed in many lands and through successive ages, led the ancient Egyptians to seek sepulture in or near the sacred spot. The smaller of the two temples was of extraordinary richness and beauty. It was built of polished granite, lined with Oriental alabaster, still glowing with the colours which adorned it nearly four thousand years ago.[2]

The larger temple, erected by Seti, the father of Ramses II., is partly buried in the sand, which, whilst it conceals, has also preserved from injury so many remains of ancient magnificence. The colossal walls and columns which have been laid bare are decorated with sculptures and paintings. They record or depict the exploits of the king. We see him treading down his

[1] Abydos claimed to be the place where the head of Osiris was buried after his dismemberment by Set. Not Philæ alone, but thirteen other places claimed that various other parts of the body of the slain god were buried in their neighbourhood, and therefore devoted themselves specially to the worship of Osiris. Abydos, however, remained from the dawn of Egyptian history to its close the supreme centre of the cult of Osiris, and the Holy City of one of the most interesting aspects of Egyptian Religion.

[2] It was from this temple that the famous tablet of Abydos was brought, which forms one of the most valuable treasures of the British Museum. The temple of Ramses II., referred to in the text, is actually built of fine-grained limestone ; but it is largely adorned with red and black granite (used for the door-frames), and alabaster (used for the shrine), while the columns are of sandstone. The reliefs of the larger temple of Seti I. are among the most notable examples of the Egyptian art of the New Empire. Behind this temple M. Naville has discovered a remarkable subterranean building, of which parts apparently date from the Pyramid-age, and which is almost unquestionably Strabo's Memnonium of Abydos, with its sacred well.

enemies at the head of his victorious armies, or worshipping the gods, or doing homage to his ancestors. In other parts of the building he is represented as eagerly engaged in the excitement of the chase, all the incidents of which are given ; amongst others, a wild bull has been lassoed, whose struggles to get free are represented with wonderful spirit.

Between Girgeh and Denderah, our next halting-place, we pass the shrine of Sheikh Selim, one of the Moslem saints who in every age have thriven upon the superstitious credulity of the Egyptians. He is believed neither to eat, drink, nor sleep, but to spend his whole time in prayer and meditation. As we approached the spot, our crew began to collect money amongst themselves. Having got together a goodly heap of piastres, they tied them up in a handkerchief, and brought the boat as near the shore as they could with safety. A gang of ruffianly-looking Arabs, the attendants of the saint, now made their appearance, and with shouts and gesticulations demanded backsheesh in the name of their master. The parcel of coin being thrown to them, a violent scuffle took place for its possession, which continued till they had reached the hut of the saint. In reply to my expression of surprise at the large amount of money collected, I was told that on their last voyage the crew had neglected to make the usual contribution, and, as a consequence, every window on board had been broken by Sheikh Selim's curse, and the boat had run aground on a mud-bank in the river, where she lay for thirty-six hours before she could be got off. Our dragoman, an unbelieving Maltese, gave me a droll account of the piles of provisions brought by the peasantry to this fasting saint, adding, with a roguish twinkle of the

CLEOPATRA AT DENDERAH.

eye, "And yet I firmly believe that he never eats any-thing—except geese and turkeys."

The great temple of Denderah is about sixty miles above Abydos. It was dedicated to Hathor, the Egyptian Venus, and belongs to the later and degraded period of architecture, when the Pharaohs had been superseded by the Ptolemies and the Cæsars. A curious interest attaches to its date. In the early part of the present century, one of the zodiacs which ornament the roof being examined by the French *savans*, was supposed to indicate an antiquity so great as to be incompatible with the Biblical narrative of the Creation and the Flood. Learned and elaborate arguments were constructed to prove that the Nile Valley must have been peopled by a highly civilised race at a period long anterior to the existence of man upon the earth as recorded in the Book of Genesis. But in their eager haste to disprove the authority of the Mosaic writings, the Egyptologists strangely overlooked the fact that the walls of the temple afford conclusive proof that, so far from going back to a mythical antiquity, it is scarcely older than the Christian era, having been commenced by Cleopatra and not completed till the reign of Nero.[1]

The vast size, the almost perfect preservation, and the sumptuous adornments of the temple make it very impressive. But it wants the severe and simple grandeur

---

[1] It should be remembered that the Biblical record, and the system of chronology which Archbishop Usher derived from it, are two very different things. There can be no doubt that the Nile Valley was peopled by a highly civilised race long before 4004 B.C. (Usher's date for the Creation), for the Egyptian Calendar was introduced by 4241 B.C. But this fact affects only Usher's chronology, not the Biblical record. In any case Dr. Manning's statement about the age of the temple is quite correct, and the Zodiac of Denderah is modern, as things go in Egypt.

of the older edifices. It is overloaded with ornament, not in the best taste, and is a formal and florid imitation of the edifices of an earlier age. Sculptured upon the walls are portraits of Cleopatra, of colossal size. They are far from supporting her reputation for beauty. The face is expressive of sensuality and voluptuousness, and bears no trace of the ambition and intelligence with which she had been credited. Their resemblance to the original has sometimes been called in question, but, as Dean Stanley remarks, " the fat full features are well brought out, and being like those at Hermonthis, give the impression that it must be a likeness."

We are now approaching Thebes, the capital of Ancient Egypt, and the culminating point of its splendour and magnificence. Throughout a period nearly twice the length of our own history the wealth and power of successive Pharaohs had been devoted to its aggrandisement, and the labour of subdued and enslaved nations been employed in the erection of its temples and palaces. For fifteen hundred years each succeeding generation added something to its glories. Its Titanic edifices record the history and illustrate the greatness of the people throughout the whole period of their national existence.[1]

The great plain of Thebes afforded a noble site for such a city. The Arabian and Libyan Mountains which

---

[1] The statement requires some modification. There are no remains of important building at Thebes earlier than the XIIth Dynasty, and even these, as in the case of the Middle Kingdom fragments at Karnak, are very scanty. The importance of Thebes really dates from the accession of the XVIIIth Dynasty in 1580 B.C. and it ceases to be the sole capital with the division of sovereignty in the XXIst Dynasty, 1090 B.C. Its period of glory, therefore, lasted almost exactly 500 years. Temple-building on a large scale went on, however, down to the end of the national story ; and in that sense Dr. Manning's allowance of 1,500 years is accurate enough.

enclose the Nile Valley here assume grander forms than
in the northern parts of the chain, and they recede farther
from the river, so as to enclose an amphitheatre of
considerable extent, through the centre of which the
river runs with a broad expanse of verdure on either
bank. Within the area enclosed by these mighty bulwarks
stood edifices, the ruins of which fill the spectator with
awe-struck wonder. Avenues of statues and sphinxes,
miles in length, ran along the plain, leading to propylons
a hundred feet in height, through which kings and
warriors, priests and courtiers, passed into the temples
and palaces which lay beyond. Above all towered the
colossal images of the Pharaohs, looking down upon the
city, and far over the plain at their feet, like gigantic
warders. As I wandered day after day with ever-growing
amazement amongst these relics of ancient magnificence,
I felt that if all the ruins in Europe—Classical, Celtic,
and Mediæval—were brought together into one centre,
they would fall far short both in extent and grandeur
of those of this single Egyptian city.

Its original name was T-Ape, the head or capital,
of which Thebes is a corruption.[1] By the Hebrews it
was known as No-Amon, the abode of Amon, the god
to whom it was specially dedicated. References to its
greatness and prophecies of its downfall are frequent
in Scripture. Among the most striking of these is that
of Nahum, when, taunting Nineveh, he says : " Art
thou better than No-Amon, that was situated by the rivers,
that had the waters round about it, whose rampart was
the sea-like stream, and whose wall was the sea-like

---

[1] This is doubtful. The Egyptian name for the city was
" Weset." " No satisfactory explanation has been offered of why the
Greeks bestowed upon it the name Thebes."

stream ? Ethiopia and Egypt were her strength, and it was infinite; Put and Lubim were her helpers. Yet she was carried away, she went into captivity." [1] The present desolation of the magnificent city affords an emphatic commentary on the denunciations of prophecy.

To depict and describe in detail the stupendous ruins which cover the great Theban plain would require many volumes like the present. We can only glance at some of the most important.

On the western bank, in what was called the Libyan suburb, stands the great temple-palace known as the Ramesseum, or Memnonium. It was built by Ramses II., whose favourite title, Mi-Amon, the beloved of Amon, was probably corrupted by the Greeks into Memnon, and in this form has passed into the languages of modern Europe. We can yet read upon its walls the achievements of the great king. We see him leading on his armies, slaughtering his enemies, receiving the spoils of captured cities, or peacefully administering his mighty empire, then co-extensive with the known world.[2] Over all towered the colossal image of Pharaoh himself. No description, no measurement, gives any adequate idea of the bulk of this enormous statue, now prostrate in the dust. It was formed out of a block of

---

[1] Thebes was sacked in 661 B.C. "When the prophet Nahum was denouncing the coming destruction of Nineveh, fifty years later, the desolation of Thebes was still fresh in his mind as he addressed the doomed city; 'Art thou better than No-Amon (Thebes), that was situate among the rivers?'" Breasted, *History of Egypt*, p. 559. The prophet was using the accomplished fact of the fall of Thebes to give point to his prediction of that of Nineveh.

[2] This takes the boastful Ramses II. too much at his own estimate. Far from being "co-extensive with the known world," the empire of Egypt had already, in his days, shrunk considerably from the limits which it had reached at the time of the culmination of the New Empire under Thothmes III. and Amenhotep III.

OSIRIDE COLUMNS OF RAMESSEUM, THEBES.

syenite granite, estimated to weigh when entire nearly nine hundred tons. It measures twenty-two feet from shoulder to shoulder ; a toe is three feet long, the foot five feet across. It is now generally agreed that this was the king who " knew not Joseph " and who so cruelly oppressed the Israelites. His mummy was discovered at Deir-el-Bahari, in 1881.[1]

Near the Ramesseum are the temples of Medinet-Abû, that is, as it should be understood, the city of Thebes. The largest of this group of buildings was erected by Ramses III., the last of the great warrior-kings of Egypt, about 1200 B.C. As in the case of his predecessors, we can trace his history on the walls of the temple. The glowing words of Lord Lindsay do not exaggerate the impressiveness of this marvellous edifice : " I will only say that all I had anticipated of Egyptian magnificence fell short of the reality, and that it was here, surveying those Osiride pillars, that splendid corridor, with its massy circular columns ; those walls lined, within and without, with historical sculpture of the deepest interest, the monarch's wars with the Eastern nations bordering on the Caspian and Bactriana—study for months, years rather !—it was here, I say, here, where almost every peculiarity of Egyptian architecture is assembled in perfection, that I first learnt to appreciate the spirit of that extraordinary people, and to feel that, poetless as they were, they *had* a national genius, and had stamped it on the works of their hands, lasting as the *Iliad*. Willing slaves to the vilest superstition, bondsmen to form and circumstance, adepts in every mechanical art that can add luxury or comfort to human existence,

[1] See Chapter IV. of this volume. The question of the Pharaoh of the Oppression is, however, by no means settled.

TEMPLE OF RAMSES III., MEDINET-ABÛ.

G

yet triumphing abroad over the very Scythians, captives from every quarter of the globe figuring in those long oblational processions to the sacred shrines in which they delighted, after returning to their native Nile— that grave, austere, gloomy architecture, sublime in outline and heavily elaborate in ornament, what a transcript was it of their own character ! And never were pages more graphic. The gathering, the march, the *mêlée*—the Pharaoh's prowess, standing erect, as he always does, in his car—no charioteer—the reins attached to his waist—the arrow drawn to his ear—his horses all fire, springing into the air like Pegasuses—and then the agony of the dying, transfixed by his darts, the relaxed limbs of the slain ; and, lastly, the triumphant return, the welcome home, and the offerings of thanksgiving to Amon, the fire, the discrimination with which these ideas are bodied forth must be seen to judge of it." [1]

Adjoining the temple are the ruins of a pyramidal tower, the internal arrangements and sculptures of which show that it was the palace of Ramses. It is remarkable as being almost the only instance yet discovered of an ancient dwelling.[2] The Egyptians built their temples and tombs for eternity. Their own

---

[1] Medinet Habu scarcely deserves Lord Lindsay's eloquent panegyric. It is XXth Dynasty architecture, belonging, that is, to a period when Egyptian art was on the down-grade, and is quite unworthy of being taken as truly representative of what the Egyptian architect could do at his best. It is one of the misfortunes which have hindered the appreciation of the great merits of Egyptian architecture that the most perfectly preserved specimen of the temples of the Empire should be, not an XVIIIth Dynasty shrine, but a XXth Dynasty one.

[2] The so-called Pavilion of Medinet-Habu, here referred to, is in no sense to be taken as a specimen of a normal Egyptian house or palace. It is a fancy structure erected by Ramses III. on his return from his Syrian Wars, and is probably a reminiscence of one of the Syrian " Migdols " or watch-towers which he had captured.

houses were constructed of perishable materials, to last only for the brief period of their continuance on earth. The rooms are small, but richly decorated. We see the king surrounded by the ladies of his court, who fan him, present him with flowers, and pay him court. In one place he is seen playing a game of chess, or draughts, with his attendants. The draught-men and the chequered board, though sculptured on the walls more than three thousand years ago, are similar to those used at the present day.

Seated in solemn and solitary majesty in the plain between the temples of Medinet-Abû and the river, are the two " Colossi." They alone remain of an avenue of eighteen similar statues which led up to the temple of Amenophis III.[1] Though much broken and shattered, they present an aspect of wonderful grandeur. The following are the measurements as given by Murray : eighteen feet three inches across the shoulders : sixteen feet six inches from the top of the shoulder to the elbow ; ten feet six inches from the top of the head to the shoulder ; seventeen feet nine inches from the elbow to the finger's end ; nineteen feet eight inches from the knee to the plant of the foot. When entire, they must have risen to a height of sixty feet. One of them was partially overthrown either by Cambyses, the great Persian conqueror, or by an earthquake ; it has, however, been restored, They were on their thrones when the Israelites were in Egypt, and they seem likely to remain there to the end of the world. One of them, known as the Vocal Memnon, was believed to emit a musical sound as the

---

[1] There is no evidence that such an avenue ever existed. On the contrary Petrie has shown (*Six Temples at Thebes*) that the avenue consisted of couchant jackals, with a statue of the King backing against each pedestal.

rays of the rising sun fell upon it, or in the presence of distinguished visitors.   Various explanations were offered of this phenomenon, such as the trickling of sand amongst the cracks of the figure, or a slight movement of its parts caused by a change of temperature.   The mystery was dispelled by Sir Gardner Wilkinson, who discovered in the lap of the figure a slab of stone, which on being struck, gives out the exact sound described by Strabo and others.[1]   For a trifling backsheesh, an Arab climbs up the statue, and, unseen by persons in the plain below, produces as often as is wished the note " like the breaking of an harp string," which was thrice repeated in honour of the Emperor Hadrian on his visit to Thebes.

Crossing the river to Luxor, which lies on the opposite bank we find an Arab village, built within and upon the temples of Amenophis III. and Ramses II.   The effect is grotesque, and detracts sorely from their impressiveness.[2]   The silence and the sense of loneliness, which elsewhere give such a weird solemnity to the ruins, are here dispelled by the miserable hovels which cluster round the stately columns, and the swarms of beggars clamorously demanding backsheesh.   There is, however, one part of the ruins remote from the village which is not infested by these annoyances, and here it is possible to admire the graceful, yet massive columns, and realise, in some measure, what Egyptian architecture was in its most perfect period of development.

The temple-palaces of Luxor and Karnak were united

[1] Among explanations which all seem inadequate, perhaps the least inadequate is the change of temperature one.
[2] The temple of Luxor has now been cleared of these disfigurements ; but the Mohammedan mosque of the village still remains a hindrance to the complete appreciation of the building.

THE COLOSSI AT THEBES.

by a magnificent avenue of sphinxes, which led for nearly
two miles across the plain. The roadway between them
was sixty-three feet in width, and as the sphinxes were

COLUMNS OF TEMPLE AT LUXOR BEFORE THE RECENT EXCAVATIONS

only twelve feet apart, the number of these majestic
figures was almost incredible. For fifteen hundred
feet from Luxor, they were of the usual form, with female

heads ; thence to Karnak they were crio, or ramheaded sphinxes, as being sacred to Amon. A similar avenue led from the main front to a quay and flight of steps on the bank of the river, and eight or ten other approaches, not inferior in grandeur to these two, have been traced.

As we approach Karnak, the most striking objects are two of the enormous pylons so characteristic of Egyptian architecture. They are truncated pyramids, pierced with a gateway. The sides slope inward from a rectangular base, and are often surmounted by a heavy cornice, on which is sculptured the symbol known to the Greeks as the *Agathodæmon,* a winged sun, or scarabæus, reminding us of the words of Scripture, " He shall cover thee with His feathers, and under His wings shalt thou trust." [1]   It was the number of these pylons which gained for Thebes the Homeric epithet of " the hundred-gated city."

We now enter the most stupendous pile of remains —we can hardly call them ruins—in the world. Every writer who has attempted to describe them, avows his inability to convey any adequate idea of their extent and grandeur. The long, converging avenues of sphinxes, the sculptured corridors, the columned aisles, the gates, and obelisks, and colossal statues, all silent in their desolation, fill the beholder with awe. There is no exaggeration in Champollion's words : " The imagination, which in Europe rises far above our porticoes, sinks abashed at the foot of the one hundred and forty columns of the hypostyle hall at Karnak." The area of this hall is fifty-seven thousand six hundred and twenty-nine feet. The central columns are thirty-four feet in circumference and sixty-two feet in height, without

[1] Psalm xci. 4.

STATUE OF RAMSES II., AT LUXOR.

reckoning the plinth and abacus. They are covered with paintings and sculptures, the colours of which are wonderfully fresh and vivid. If, as seems probable, the great design of Egyptian architecture was to impress man with a feeling of his own littleness, to inspire a sense of overwhelming awe in the presence of the deity, and, at the same time, to show that the monarch was a being of superhuman greatness, these edifices were well adapted to accomplish their purpose. This has been well stated by Mr. Zincke in his suggestive work on Egypt. The Egyptian beholder and worshipper was not to be attracted and charmed, but overwhelmed. His own nothingness, and the terribleness of the power and will of God, were what he was to feel. But if the awfulness of the deity was thus inculcated, the divine power of the Pharaoh was not less strikingly set forth. He is seen seated amongst the gods, nourished from their breast, folded in their arms, admitted to familiar inter-course with them. He is represented on the walls of the temples as of colossal stature, whilst the noblest of his subjects are but pigmies in his presence. With one hand he crushes hosts of enemies, with the other he grasps that of his patron and deity. The Pharaoh was the earthly manifestation and *avatar* of the unseen and mysterious power which oppressed the souls of men with terror. " I am Pharaoh ; " " by the life of Pharaoh ; " " say unto Pharaoh, Whom art thou like in thy greatness ? " [1] These familiar phrases of Scripture gain a new emphasis of meaning as we remember them amongst these temple-palaces. It is with a feeling of relief that we turn away from these dread-inspiring deities to think

---

[1] Genesis xli. 44 ; xlii. 15, 16 ; Ezekiel xxxii. 2. Quoted by Dean Stanley, in *Sinai and Palestine*.

AMEN LEADING UP SHISHAK'S CAPTIVES, ON SCULPTURED WALL AT KARNAK.

of Him who " dwelleth not in temples made with hands ; "
who calls Himself our Father, and who invites from us
not the servile worship of terror, but a filial " love which
casteth out fear : " whose earthly manifestation and
incarnation has been made, not in the person of a deified
conqueror, but in one who was " a Man of sorrows and
acquainted with grief ; " who " is touched with a feeling
of our infirmities ; " who " bare our sins in His own
body on the tree," and who is now exalted to the right
hand of the Majesty on high, " a Prince and a Saviour,
to give repentance and the remission of sins."

Amongst the temples of Karnak a special interest
attaches to one comparatively late in date, but which is
the earliest yet discovered which directly and certainly
touches the history of other nations. Sheshank—the
Shishak of Scripture—was one of the last of the Pharaohs
who, for the space of more than a thousand years, had
been busy building up the glories of Karnak. He erected
a kind of chapel flanking the great portico toward the
south, and, after the manner of his race, cut into its
walls a record of his achievements. We see the colossal
figure leading in bonds the pigmy monarchs whom he
had conquered.[1] On a cartouche is written, in hieroglyphics, the name of each. The sculptures, discovered
and deciphered by Champollion, record that Shishak is
dragging before the Theban trinity the types of more
than thirty nations which he had subdued. From the
variety of their features, they are evidently intended to
be typical of the people represented. Amongst them is
one with a distinctly Jewish cast of face. Turning to

---

[1] The colossal figure is that, not of Sheshank, but of the God Amen,
who is leading up the captive cities before the never finished and
now obliterated figure of Sheshank.

the Bible, we find that, " In the fifth year of king Rehoboam, Shishak king of Egypt came up against Jerusalem, because they had transgressed against the Lord, with twelve hundred chariots, and threescore thousand horsemen, and people without number, and he took the fenced cities which pertained to Judah, and came to Jerusalem, and he took away the treasures of the house of the Lord, and the treasures of the king's house ; he took all." [1] This monument is thus a contemporary record of the event narrated in Scripture.

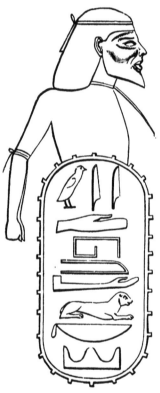

A CAPTIVE JEW OF SHISHAK'S TIME.

It has been already mentioned that the Egyptians built their houses of perishable materials, but that their temples and tombs were constructed on the grandest scale, and of the most enduring character. How true this is of the Theban temples we have seen. We now turn to the tombs, which are scarcely less wonderful in their extent and magnificence. They were constructed in the *háger*, that is, " a rock," and refers to the rocky

[1] 1 Kings xiv. 25 ; 2 Chron. xii. 3–9

TEMPLE OF QUEEN HATSHEPSUT,

DER EL-BAHRI.

precipices which rise from the fertile banks of the river. Crossing the western plain, here about three miles in width, and leaving behind us the seated Colossi, and the temples of Kûrnah, Medinet-Abû, and the Ramesseum, we enter a savage gorge. The walls of rock on either side of the ravine, utterly denuded of soil, glow in the pitiless sunshine, like the mouth of a furnace. Overhead rises a pyramidal mass of rock, which forms a striking feature in the landscape, and commands from its summit a striking view of the Nile Valley and Desert. No tree, or blade of grass, or drop of water, or living thing is visible as the travellers pass along in the blind glare. This gorge leads us to the Bibán el Moluk, or Tombs of the Kings. The rocks are honeycombed with sepulchres, which run far into the mountain sides. Here the Theban Pharaohs " lie in glory, every one in his own house." [1] Near them are queens, priests, and nobles, interred with a splendour not inferior to that of the Pharaohs. Some of these sepulchral halls are of vast extent. One of them, that of the Assaseef, is eight hundred and sixty-two feet in length, without reckoning the lateral chambers ; the total area of excavation is twenty-three thousand eight hundred and nine feet, occupying an acre and a quarter of ground, " an immoderate space for the sepulchre of one individual, even allowing that the members of his family shared a portion of its extent." [2]

The sides of these tombs are covered with frescoes and sculptures, sometimes giving the portrait of the

[1] Isaiah xiv. 18.
[2] This is the tomb of Pedu-amen-apt, an official under the XXVIth Dynasty. It is more than double the length of the most famous royal tomb in the Valley of the Kings, that of Sety I., but is now inaccessible.

inmate and illustrating his career. More frequently, they are fancy sketches, or what we should call *genre* paintings. The life of the Egyptian people is here

FRESCO IN TOMB OF THE KINGS AT THEBES.

portrayed with extraordinary accuracy and detail. " We saw here, as in a picture story-book, how the man had cultivated his garden and fields, had garnered his harvests,

FRESCO IN TOMB OF THE KINGS AT THEBES.

had sent merchandise on the river in boats sailing with the wind—how he had gone to battle and taken the command of armies—the gathering in of his vintage,

the games and shoutings of the wine-pressers, his sports
in fishing and fowling. Then we saw him—a picture
of easy joy—in the midst of the family circle. We saw
him at the feast : guests were at his dwelling ; he wel-
comed them to the merry banquet ; slaves crowned them
with garlands of flowers ; the wine-cup passed round.

HARPER IN TOMB AT THEBES.

Then there were harpers and musicians and players on
the double pipes. Girls in long wavy hair and light
clinging garments were dancing. But to all things there
comes an end. We saw here, also, the day (how far
back in the depths of time !) when these pleasant feasts
were all over—the lilies dead, the music hushed, the
last of this man's harvest stored, the last trip enjoyed

by boat or chariot. The fish need no more fear him in the pools, nor the fowl among the reeds. Here he was lying under the hands of the embalmers. And next we saw him in mummy form on the bier, in the consecrated boat which was to carry him over the dark river and land him at the gates of the heavenly abode, where the genii of the dead and Osiris were awaiting him to try his deeds, and pronounce his sentence for eternal good or ill." [1]

Standing among the affecting memorials of lives, the earthly course of which was terminated thousands of years ago, we ask ourselves, what knowledge or hope had they of the life to come ? They distinctly recognised the great facts of a judgment after death, the immortality of the soul, and the resurrection of the body. The practice of embalming the dead was indeed but an expression of this belief, which was wrought into their whole habit of thought and mode of life. We learn this not merely from the inscriptions in the tombs, temples, and on the sarcophagi, but from rolls of papyrus placed with the mummy in the coffin, which trace the course of the disembodied spirit to the regions of reward or punishment. In one chapter of these Books of the Dead, as they are called, we see the spirit hovering over the corpse in the form of a hawk, with human head and hands, and grasping the symbol of life and stability. The body is borne across the river, accompanied by priests and mourners to the grave. The spirit passes away to *Amenti*. Here it encounters innumerable perils from the monsters which lie in wait to avenge upon it any crimes of which it has been guilty during life. The prayers and protestations of innocence which are to

[1] *Leisure Hour*, May, 1867.

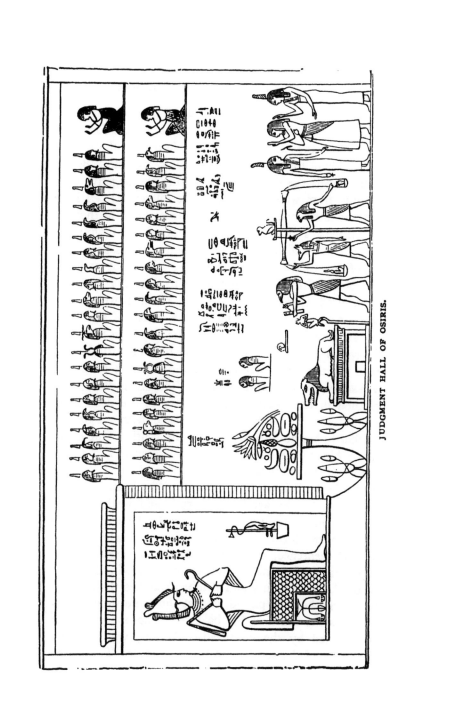

JUDGMENT HALL OF OSIRIS.

prove its safeguard are dictated. Then it enters the judgment hall of Osiris. Here are seen the forty-two judges of the dead. Some are human, others have the heads of the crocodile, hawk, lion, ape, etc. Before them kneels the dead man, repeating the negative confession, from which we extract the following : " I have defrauded no man : I have not prevaricated at the seat of justice : I have not made slaves of the Egyptians : I have not defiled my conscience for the sake of my superior : I have not used violence : I have not famished my household : I have not made to weep : I have not committed forgery : I have not falsified weights or measures : I have not pierced the banks of the Nile, nor separated for myself an arm of the Nile in its increase : I have not been gluttonous : I have not been drunken : " etc. In the lower tier is the judgment hall of Osiris. We see on the right three figures. The one in the centre, clothed in the usual Egyptian dress, is the dead man. He is received by two females, each with an ostrich feather in her headdress, symbolising Truth. One introduces him to the other, who holds a sceptre and a *crux ansata*—the symbols of authority and life. In the centre is the balance of judgment. The heart is placed in one scale, the symbols of truth and justice in the other. One of the ministers of Thoth, the scribe of the gods, in the form of a dog-headed ape, whose name is Hap (sentence, judgment), sits on the stand which supports the balance. Horus, the hawk-headed, the beloved son of Osiris and Anubis, watches the scale in which the heart is placed, and at the same time closely observes the index of the balance. The opposite scale is trimmed by the dog-headed Anubis, who declares the result of the scrutiny to the ibis-headed Thoth, the divine wisdom, who stands with his writing-tablet and pen in front of Osiris, the supreme judge of this fearful assize, and records the sentence in his presence. Osiris himself is seated in a shrine on the extreme left, and wears a diadem adorned with two ostrich feathers, and with the disk of the sun and the horns of a goat. He holds a whip and a crook-headed sceptre, symbolising

SOUL VISITING ITS BODY, AND HOLDING THE EMBLEMS
OF LIFE AND BREATH IN ITS CLAWS.

justice and law. Immediately before the throne, and within the shrine, is a stand, upon which is hung the skin of a panther: the meaning of this is unknown. An altar laden with offerings, and surmounted by the lotus-flower, stands in front of the shrine. It probably represents the acts of piety performed on behalf of the deceased by his surviving relatives. On the pedestal before the throne a monster crouches, with the paws of

H

a lion and the head of a crocodile and the body of a horse ; [1] his name, " the Devourer of Amenti," as well as his appearance, point him out as another of the ministers of vengeance executing the judgments of the divinity before whom he crouches.

The sentence pronounced was full of joy to the good, and of woe to the wicked. They who, by the faithful discharge of their duties as children, as parents, as masters or servants, as kings or subjects, had been enabled to pass the ordeal, were admitted to the habitations of blessedness, where they rested from their labours. Here they reap the corn and gather the fruits of paradise under the eye and smile of the lord of joy, that is, the sun, who exhorts them thus : " Take your sickles, reap your grain, carry it into your dwellings, and be glad therewith, and present it a pure offering to the god." There also they bathe in the pure river of life that flows past their habitations. Over them is inscribed : " They have found favour in the eyes of the great god, they inhabit the mansions of glory, where they enjoy the life of heaven ; the bodies which they have abandoned shall repose in their tombs while they rejoice in the presence of the supreme god."

The system of eschatology, thus sketched in the briefest possible outline, suggests many questions of profound interest, to which, however, no adequate reply can at present be given. Whence was it derived ? Is it a distorted tradition of some primeval revelation made to man ; or is it but a part of that universal illumination of the Holy Spirit, which " enlightening every man

---

[1] The head is crocodile, the fore part of the body, panther, the hinder part hippopotamus. The monster's name is Ammit, and its function is to be the devourer of the unjustified.

that cometh into the world," never leaves God without
a witness even in the heart of the heathen, " so that they
are without excuse " ? It is easy for us to discover a
symbolism in the forms in which these beliefs were
embodied. For instance, we may see in the monsters
which avenged the different vices and crimes upon
offenders, the types of those vices and crimes themselves,
thus suggesting the truth that those sins brought with
them their own punishment. How far did the Egyptians
understand these deeper and more spiritual teachings ?
This doctrine of a future state of rewards and punish-
ments was fully developed at the time when Moses was
" learned in all the wisdom of the Egyptians." It must
have been known to him. How comes it, then, that
truths which hold so prominent a place in the later
Scriptures, should be almost, or altogether, passed over
in his writings ? This is one of those unexplained
silences of Scripture for the explanation of which we
must wait in faith and patience. We cannot but note
yet further the insufficiency of the knowledge thus
possessed to bring peace and pardon to the guilty. The
ritual of the dead tells us that the innocent man shall
be " justified " in the judgment hall of Osiris. " Where,
then, shall the sinner and the ungodly appear ? " It
was reserved for Him who " brought life and immortality to light," and who " gave Himself a ransom
for us," to reveal the way of the sinner's acceptance
with God through faith in Him " that justifieth the
ungodly."

Before leaving the tombs at Thebes, it is necessary
to refer to one which is supposed to contain a record
of the captivity of the Israelites in Egypt. A gang of
slaves are engaged in brickmaking, under the eye of a

task-master, who is seated, staff in hand, superintending their labours. That they belong to a Semitic race is evident. But that the Jews were ever settled so high up in the Nile Valley is very doubtful. Pithom and Raamses, the treasure cities which they are said to have built, were on the north-eastern frontier in the Land of Goshen,[1] and their name does not occur amongst those of the nations recorded in this tomb. The painting is, however, interesting as illustrating the condition of a people compelled " to serve with rigour in mortar and in brick, and in all manner of service in the field." [2]

Leaving Thebes reluctantly, and feeling that months might be spent in exploring its remains, we pursue our course up the Nile, and reach Esneh. Here is a temple, the portico of which has been excavated only in the nineteenth century. The sand in which it was so long buried preserved its sculptures and paintings in marvellous perfection. The colours are as fresh and bright as when laid on at the commencement of the Christian era. It belongs to the later period of Egyptian art, when it had come decidedly under Greek influence. The present edifice probably occupies the site of an older one, built by Thothmes III. The palm leaf here replaces the lotus in the capitals of the columns, which are of great beauty. No two are alike. Their variety and grace afford a fine study for the decorative artist. We may observe here the change which had passed over the Egyptian feeling towards the gods and Pharaohs, since the time when they were regarded with awe and terror. Greek thought and feeling had humanised the deities, and brought them down from their mysterious seclusion

[1] Exodus i. 11.　　　　[2] Exodus i. 13, 14.

PORTICO AND TEMPLE OF ESNEH.

into friendly intercourse with man. In one panel we see them assisting the monarchs in the sports of the field. They are holding the cords of a clapnet in four divisions. The upper tier encloses flying birds ; the second, birds perched among the trees ; the third, water-fowl ; the fourth, fishes. In another section, the gods, with their characteristic head-dresses and symbols of authority, are driving bulls, goats, and flocks of geese. Whilst the form of Egyptian worship remained, the sense of reverence and awe, which formed its spirit and essence, had departed.

About thirty miles above Esneh is the most perfectly preserved temple in Egypt—that of Edfu. Until excavated by M. Mariette, in 1864, only the propylons were visible ; the rest was hidden beneath an Arab village which had been built upon its walls and sanctuary. It belongs to the period of the Ptolemies, and, like the temple at Esneh, exhibits the gods engaged in field-sports. One corridor is mainly devoted to harpooning the hippopotamus, and, with the irresistible tendency of the Egyptians to caricature, many of the incidents are very droll. In several cases the clumsy harpooner has struck his weapon into one of the attendants, instead of the animal at which it was aimed. Doubtless there was a mythological meaning in the sculptures—the hippopotamus being a symbol of Typhon, the Evil principle. But the realism and the fun of the scene are strangely out of keeping with the conventional and reverential tone of earlier art.

A few hours after leaving Edfu we reach Silsileh, which is interesting as being the quarry from which the stone was cut for the temples and palaces of Thebes. The excavations are of immense extent on both sides or the river, which is here very narrow. They have been vividly described by Eliot Warburton, who says : "Hollowed out of the rocks are squares as large as that of St. James's, streets as large as Pall Mall, and lanes and alleys without number ; in short, you have all the negative features of a town, if I may so speak, *i.e.*, if a town be considered as a *cameo*, these quarries are a vast *intaglio*." The tool-marks of the masons, made three thousand years ago, are distinctly visible, and it is easy to see the methods employed to separate the huge blocks of stone, in the absence of gun-powder or other explosive material. Wooden wedges were inserted into the rock, and then moistened. As the line of wedges swelled, a mass of stone was detached of the size required. Remembering the stir and bustle of which these quarries were once the scene, their present solitude and silence are most impressive. Facing the river are a number of small grottoes or chapels, apparently for the use of the quarrymen, and these, with the buttresses of stone carved into the form of columns, have a very picturesque appearance, giving the impression of a vast city hewn out of the living rock.

Fifteen miles above Silsileh, we reach the temple of Kom Ombo. Standing as it does on the summit of a hill overlooking the Nile Valley, it forms a very striking object from the river. Though small in size as compared with the mighty masses of Karnak and Luxor, it is one of the most beautiful edifices in Egypt. The sand-drift from the desert has buried the lower part of the columns, and threatens to submerge the whole. On the river-side the banks are being rapidly undermined by the force of the current. One smaller temple lower down the slope has already been swept away, and apparently in a few years this too will disappear.[1]

We now approach the first cataract of the Nile. The scenery begins to assume a more distinctively Nubian character. Soon the ruined towers over Assouan come into view, and the second stage of our journey is completed.

---

[1] The temple of Kom Ombo is now protected from the destruction which threatened it by an embankment.

CHAPTER III

ASSOUAN TO ABU-SIMBEL

THE approach to Assouan is very picturesque, and affords a pleasing contrast to the scenery of the Lower and Middle Nile. Instead of flat monotonous banks of sand and mud, we have masses of rock, broken up into grotesque and fantastic forms. Groves of palm, mimosa, and castor-oil plant come down to the water's edge. The limestone and sandstone ranges which hem in the Nile Valley from Cairo to Silsileh, give place to granite, porphyry, and basalt. The islands in the stream are no longer shifting accretions of mud, alternately formed and dissolved by the force of the current, but rocks and boulders of granite, which rise high above the river and resist its utmost force. The ruined convents and towers which crown the hills might almost cheat us into the belief that we were afloat on the Rhine or the Moselle, but for the tropical character of the scenery.

This altered aspect of the scenery is in accordance with the political geography of the district. We have reached the southern boundary of Egypt, and are about to enter Nubia. The kingdom of the Pharaohs lies behind us, and we are on the borderland from which they marched for the conquest of Ethiopia. To this fact Ezekiel refers when, denouncing the Divine vengeance against Egypt, he says : " Behold, therefore, I am against thee, and against thy rivers, and I will make the land of Egypt utterly waste and desolate, from Migdol to Syene, even the border of Ethiopia." [1]

Assouan is a great centre for traffic with the interior. Caravans arrive from the desert, the camels are unloaded, and in a few days start again with consignments of manufactured articles—prints, beads, guns, powder—for barter with the native tribes. Dhows from Nubia and the Soudan, too heavily laden to descend the cataract, discharge their cargoes near Philæ, to be borne overland to this point for transhipment to Cairo or Alexandria. A broad open space outside the town, on the bank of the river, serves at once as warehouse and exchange. Arabs, Turks, Negroes, Nubians, Abyssinians meet here on a footing of perfect equality. Trade levels all distinctions. Many of them are camped in native fashion. Bales of goods are arranged in a circle, so as to form a rampart against attack. In the centre a fire is kindled for cooking, around which the women and children lounge, whilst the men are chaffering in the bazaars, or gossiping on the beach. All the products of Central Africa may be bought here—elephants' tusks, odoriferous gums, ostrich feathers, ebony, clubs, poisoned arrows, shields of rhinoceros hide, strange birds, monkeys, and sometimes lions. I was asked fifteen pounds for a lion cub, about the size of a Newfoundland dog. Failing to find a purchaser, the owner gradually came down to four pounds ; but it remained unsold. It was a good-tempered little brute, playing about like a huge

---

[1] Ezekiel xxix. 10, *margin*. Migdol was the frontier town on the north-east, as Syene, or Assouan, was on the south.

over-grown kitten, but an angry growl and ominous showing of the teeth gave warning of trouble at no distant period.

Opposite Assouan is the Island of Elephantine, or, as it is called by the natives, Geziret ez Zaher, the Island of Flowers. It formed an outpost for the successive lords of Egypt—Pharaohs, Ptolemies, Cæsars, and Saracen Caliphs—all of whom have left traces of their military occupation. The temples and the Nilometer, which, up to 1822, stood on the island, have almost disappeared, having been used as a quarry by the Governor of Assouan to build himself a palace. Only a few fragments now remain to excite our indignation against the vandalism of the destroyer.

In continuing our journey from Assouan and Elephantine to Philæ, we may either ride across the desert or ascend the cataract. If we adopt the former route, we shall probably have our first experience of camel-riding, and it will be far from agreeable. The animal has a peculiar gait, lifting both feet on the same side together, instead of the near fore-leg and off hind-leg, like the horse. This gives a peculiar corkscrew motion to the spine of the rider, which becomes absolutely painful after a short time. Immediately on leaving the town we pass the old Saracenic cemetery. Like all those of Modern Egypt, it is in a state of extreme neglect and dilapidation. The dead are covered with a thin sprinkling of earth, scarcely sufficient to protect them from the ravages of hyenas and jackals. The modern burial-places thus offer a striking contrast to the imperishable monuments in which the embalmed bodies were deposited by the ancient Egyptians. We soon reach the quarries from which the huge blocks of syenite granite were hewn for the temples of Lower Egypt. As at Silsileh, the quarry marks of the workmen are yet distinctly visible, and the vast extent of the excavations gives an impressive sense of the scale upon which the old builders worked. An obelisk yet remains in the quarry; it is about a hundred feet in height, by eleven feet two inches in breadth. When, and by whom it was cut out from the rock, and why it was left here instead of being removed to its destined site, cannot now be known.[1] A similar mass of stone, hewn, squared, and prepared for removal, is found in the quarries near Baalbec.

The road now enters a savage defile, even more stern and desolate than that leading to the Tombs of the Kings at Thebes. Bare granite rocks rise on either hand. The bed of the *wady* is strewn with granite boulders lying in wild confusion, many of them inscribed with hieroglyphics and sculptures. Traces of ruined fortifications are visible, intended either to protect traders

---

[1] The undetached obelisk of the Aswan quarry has been completely uncovered by Mr. R. Engelbach, acting for the Egyptian Service of Antiquities. Its actual dimensions are as follows: Length, 137 feet; Breadth at Base, 13 feet 9 inches; Breadth at Base of Pyramidion, 8 feet 2 inches; Height of Pyramidion, 14 feet 9 inches; Weight if it had been extracted, 1,168 tons. Mr. Engelbach has published the results of his researches in *The Problem of the Obelisks*, a volume full of deeply interesting details and suggestions as to the methods by which the ancient Egyptians worked and transported these gigantic blocks of stone. The Aswan obelisk was abandoned in the quarry because of the existence of fissures in the granite which rendered its completion impossible. Probably, but not certainly, it dates from the time of the XVIIIth Dynasty. Mr. Engelbach's investigations show that the great block was not split off from the rock by the action of wetted wooden wedges, as described in Dr. Manning's comments on the quarries of Silsileh, but was cut, or rather to use the explorer's own word " bashed," out by the action of a large number of rammers, capped with balls of dolerite. Numbers of the dolerite balls which formed the heads of the rammers are found in the quarry near the great obelisk, some of them fractured by the hard service to which they were put.

PORTICO OF TEMPLE AT PHILÆ.

from the attack of marauding Bedouin, or to close the pass against invading hordes from the south. Emerging from the defile of rock and sand, and crossing a strip of desert, we reach the banks of the river above the cataract. A clump of magnificent sycamores affords grateful shade after a hot and weary ride, and Philæ, with its exquisite loveliness, more than fulfils our highly raised expectations.

Before describing the other route to Philæ, it is necessary to explain that by the Cataracts of the Nile, all that is meant is a series of rapids which rush down from just below the Island of Biggeh, to just above Elephantine. There is no actual cascade or cataract, in our sense of the word, but the river boils and rages along the narrow channel, and whirls in dangerous eddies around the rocks and islets which obstruct its course. From the language of Cicero and Seneca it seems probable that two thousand years ago the fall was greater than it is now. After making allowance for the exaggerations into which classical writers fell when describing strange and unfamiliar scenes, it is difficult to suppose that they only saw what we now see.

If the river be not too low, and the wind be fair, there is abundant excitement, but no real danger, in the ascent of the cataracts. The dahabiyeh sails smoothly on between the rocky islets above Elephantine till the first rapid is reached. This is commonly passed without any difficulty, if there be a good steady breeze. It is at the second rapid that the struggle begins. The rowers strain at the oars till they bend almost to breaking. Long poles are thrust out against every rock in the channel to gain a purchase. The boatmen leap into the seething cauldron to carry a rope to some projecting headland, whence they may haul the vessel against the current.

The *reis* shouts and gesticulates to the crew like a mad-man. Sometimes the boat is caught in an eddy, whirled round, and seems to be on the point of destruction, but a shifting of the broad lateen sail, a turn of the helm, or the coiling of a rope round a mass of rock makes all right again. It is a scene of indescribable confusion. Everybody is bawling at the top of his voice. The orders of the *reis* are drowned in the hurly-burly. At length, by dint of poling and warping, the top of the rapid is reached, and the vessel floats in smooth water once again. The current still runs strong, and vigorous rowing is needed for some distance, till we find ourselves off the village of Mahatta, and close upon the temple-crowned island which is our destination.

Scarcely less exciting than the ascent of the rapids by a dahabiyeh, is the sight of the Nubians descending them. The people of the district ordinarily cross the river astride on a log of wood. Even little children paddle themselves to and fro with marvellous skill. Stripping off their clothing, if they have any, and making it up into a bundle to carry on their heads, they move about in the water as though it were their native element. Afloat in the river on these rude aboriginal rafts, a score of men will let themselves be drawn down by the current into the maddest rush and whirl of the rapid, and having reached its foot, swim ashore and beg for backsheesh, which is seldom refused.[1]

The Island of Philæ, which lies just above the first cataract, was sacred to Osiris, the most prominent figure in the Egyptian Pantheon.[2] The legends concerning

[1] The foaming rapids of the First Cataract are now, since the erection of the great dam, things of the past.

[2] The chief deity worshipped at Philæ was Isis, to whom the Great Temple was dedicated ; but her husband, Osiris, was also

him formed the centre of the Egyptian mythological
system.

The island is covered with temples, but none of
them are older than the era of the Ptolemies. The
original edifices were destroyed by Persian iconoclasts,
and very few traces of them can be discovered. It is

KHONSU.   MUT.   AMEN.

difficult to make out the general plan of the buildings.
What Sir Gardner Wilkinson called the " symmetro-
phobia " of the Egyptians is here most strikingly
illustrated. Where a modern architect would secure a

worshipped, together with Khnum and Satet, the male and female
deities of the Cataract, and there were also shrines to Hathor, to
Imhotep, the deified architect of King Zeser of the IIIrd Dynasty,
and to other divinities.

magnificent vista by avenues leading in straight lines to a central and commanding point, they broke up the ground-plan into detached and unsymmetrical portions. No part of the edifice corresponded in design to any other part. Propylons, gateways, side-chapels, seem to have been placed just where the whim of the builder

HEAD OF BES.

dictated, with little or no regard to the production of an harmonious and well-balanced whole. This is specially true of the edifices on Philæ.

The most conspicuous building on the island is a hypæthral hall, near the landing-place, vulgarly known as Pharaoh's Bed. It is detached from the main temple, and its builder and purpose are alike unknown. It can hardly have been a temple, and may possibly have been erected merely as an architectural feature. The most probable view is that it was a comparatively modern erection over the assumed grave of Osiris. Its situation is very striking, and it harmonises well with the surrounding scenery ; but I should hardly go the length of Mr. Fairholt, who pronounces it " the most exquisite in its effect of any in Egypt." [1]

The great temple of Isis was approached by a quay and a flight of steps leading up from the river at the southern end of the island. The visitor then passed between a pair of obelisks, of which only one is now standing, and along an avenue of Isis-headed columns to the great propylon. A peristyle court and a small temple, sacred to Horus, are then entered ; another smaller propylon succeeds, and we reach the grand portico of the temple of Isis, its columns glowing with colour, their capitals delicately and exquisitely designed from lotus, acacia, and palm leaves. This general plan, however, fails to give any idea of the bewildering mazes of corridors, halls, and shrines, which succeed one another. Perhaps the most interesting portion of the building is a small chapel constructed upon the roof of one of the terraces. The sculptures in this chamber represent the history of Osiris. We see the mangled remains of the slain monarch brought together, women are weeping round his bier, whilst the symbol of the soul

---

[1] Philæ, unfortunately, can no longer be seen as Dr. Manning describes it. The erection and subsequent heightening of the great Barrage has resulted in the almost complete submergence, for a considerable portion of each year, of the beautiful island and its temples. Great care has been taken to ensure that the security of the buildings shall not be compromised by their submergence, and it should be remembered that none of the temples concerned is really of ancient date, as things go in Egypt ; but the beauty of Philæ has been the price paid for the prosperity of Egypt.

hovers over the corpse.   Gradually the signs of returning
life are indicated.   Winged figures, like the cherubim
of Scripture, stand around, overshadowing and guarding
the body with their wings.   The mystic legend unfolds

PHILÆ.

itself step by step, till Osiris is seen robed, crowned,
seated upon his throne, bearing in his hands, which are
crossed upon his breast, the insignia of empire, and he
is installed as the mighty and beneficent ruler of the
invisible world.

On the downfall of the Egyptian mythology, Philæ became an important Christian colony. The monks who settled here, like those at Beni Hassan, defaced the symbols of the old faith and substituted for them those of Christianity. Some of these are very curious. We have not only the cross of the ordinary form with the familiar addition of the palm branch of victory, or enclosed within a circle of amaranth, symbolising eternity, but we find strange combinations of unusual forms with fanciful additions, of which it is often difficult to discover the meaning. Thus the Jerusalem cross, as it is now called, appears with a semicircle on each of its arms, or with globes at each extremity and grouped round the centre. What looks at first like a mere arabesque or geometrical pattern resolves itself into a series of crosses, with that of St. Andrew in the centre, and triangles at each corner, as types of the Trinity. At this distance of time it is impossible to say how far these rude inscriptions were expressive of a true spiritual faith in the Divine verities thus symbolised. But from what we know of the character of the Egyptian monks, there is but too much reason to fear that they only represent a gross superstition scarcely more respectable than the heathenism they replaced. One great cause of the rapid spread of Mohammedanism in the seventh century was the idolatry and degraded superstition into which the Church had then fallen. And at the present day one main hindrance to the progress of Christianity amongst the Moslems is their deep-rooted belief that it is essentially idolatrous—a belief created and fostered by the creed and ritual of the Greek, Latin, and Coptic Churches. Slowly this erroneous idea is being dispelled by the teaching of Protestant evangelists. But

CHRISTIAN SYMBOLS AT PHILÆ.

everywhere throughout the Mohammedan world I have found that the worship of the crucifix, of Mary, and of the saints, has raised an almost insuperable prejudice against Christianity. Strange that a faith which teaches that " God is a Spirit : and they that worship Him must worship Him in spirit and in truth," should, by the misrepresentations of its avowed adherents, have been exposed to such a charge.

The general aspect of Nubian scenery is similar to that of Egypt, but with some marked differences. The Nile flows on through a valley with mountain ranges on either hand. Its banks, fertilised by the river, are of a rich emerald green. Beyond this narrow strip of verdure all is bare rock and barren sand. But the mountain-sides are more precipitous, and come down nearer to the water's edge, thus diminishing the area to which the annual inundation rises, and, as a consequence, the cultivable soil is proportionately less. Artificial irrigation becomes more than ever needful, and sâkiyehs and shâdûfs are seen all along the river banks. The population is scanty. The soil, indeed, is wonderfully productive, but there is so little of it, that large numbers are compelled to emigrate to Cairo or Alexandria, and find employment as water-carriers donkey-drivers, or labourers. The cottages are often mere walls of baked mud, covered with thatch, with only a single chamber in each. Some of the sheikhs' houses, however, are very picturesque, and are built in the curious fashion which we have seen in Upper Egypt. The upper parts are ornamented with bands of plaster cornices, and rows of earthen pots are let into the walls, to serve as pigeon-houses.

The landscape has been gradually becoming more

tropical in character, so that we actually enter the tropics a little way above Philæ without being conscious of any marked change. Doum-palms, which we first saw just below Thebes, are striking features in the landscape. Some of them attain great size, and afford an agreeable contrast to the bare columnar stems of the date-palm. Fields of maize, millet, cotton, and sugar-cane line the banks, and produce three harvests in the year, with little toil to the cultivator, beyond that required for raising water from the river for purposes of irrigation. Most of the work in the fields is done by women and children. The men have either gone down into Egypt, or are working on the banks of the river, or are gossiping under the pleasant shade of the palms. The old women are at home minding the babies, or grinding corn, or baking bread. The young girls are busy in the fields picking cotton, or reaping, or sowing the seed for the next harvest. It is at the wayside well that the life of the people may be best seen. A pleasant picture of the groups which gather there has been drawn by Howard Hopley in the *Leisure Hour*.

"We lay hidden one day beneath a screen of inter-twisted palm fronds, dreamily lapped in a kind of doze —a slumbrous feeling communicated, I believe, by watching the shameful inactivity of a tribe of birds in their twilight cloisters above of boughs swinging gently in the lazy airs of summer's noon,—birds that manifestly toiled not for their living, but took it on trust, flaunting themselves in the most gorgeous plumage imaginable, and neither singing, nor even chatting, for the matter of that. We were lying here, I say, when we espied through our leafy screen the advent of some travellers. A mother and two children—a chubby unclad urchin of two or

ENTRANCE OF THE TEMPLE OF DAKKEH.

three, and an elder sister—entered from the outer glare and squatted down in the golden light filtering from above on to the sandy area of the grove. They could not have travelled far, for they came in so gladsome and fresh. The daughter, a fine grown girl of twelve, ran off to the well and tripped back playfully, with one hand daintily steadying an earthen bowl, dripping over with the grateful drink. Her mother awaited it, her back against a palm, in the attitude of *Judæa Capta* on the Roman coin. How these Nubian faces flash out sometimes an intelligence that no one would give them credit for ! This woman, under thirty, perhaps, yet already old and wrinkled, might have been handsome enough once, but the expression of her face was dull and stolid —of the earth earthy. Yet as she sat there straining her little blackamoor to her breast, the soul came up in her face, and she looked positively beautiful. It was like lighting the candle within the lantern. She wore a tunic of camel-hair fabric, Nubian fashion, looped up on each shoulder, leaving the arms bare. It had more the cut of the Greek palla, than the skirt of the Egyptian fellah —a kind of extra fold falling from the neck to the waist. The daughter, a pretty little woman, lissom and shapely, you might have taken for a dryad of the wood. Just budding into the woman, she retained all the playfulness of the child, and romped free in the changing leafy lights of this copse, as if her life were all play. There was something so gracious and winsome about her that you could not find heart to cavil. Yet her hair was reeking with castor oil, and I am afraid the gloss on her supple limbs was attributable to that same unguent. She seemed almost perfect in form ; and the hair in question, which fell in a hundred little plaits about her shoulders (shortened in a line across the forehead), framed a face of which the big black eyes, pouted lips, and placid mien, seemed an echo of those sweet faces you see pictured in the old tombs—an echo from a far-back world. Her sole dress, save a necklace or two of beads, was a short petticoat of tiny strips of leather, a kind of fringe decked out coquettishly with a multitude of cowry shells and glass beads, all of which tinkled merrily as she skipped along. You could not, for the life of you, call it an immodest costume, the thing was so natural and innocent. Indeed, in this country, until girls marry, such is their only dress, save a slight veil thrown over the head against the sun."

Though Nubia did not form part of Egypt proper, yet at the present day it more closely resembles the Egypt of the Pharaohs than does the region of the Lower Nile. Cut off from the rest of the world by the cataract on the north, and by the desert on the east and west, its population has been kept pure from the intermixture of foreign blood, and its manners and customs have remained almost unchanged. Faces are depicted on the monuments which might pass for portraits of those whom we see around us. The contour of the features is precisely the same. This likeness is rendered more obvious by a similarity in the mode of dressing the hair, which is arranged in small corkscrew curls, kept close to the head by saturation with castor-oil. The necklaces, ear-rings, and bracelets are the same as worn three or four thousand years ago. In any Nubian hut, wooden pillows or head-rests may be found whose form is absolutely undistinguishable from those which may be seen in the British Museum, brought there from Theban tombs.

The temples of Nubia are even more numerous than those of Egypt. But being placed there by foreign rulers as trophies of their victories, they have little historical importance, and, except those of Abu-Simbel, present few remarkable features. That of Dandour is of the Roman period, and was founded in the reign of Augustus. It is curious as an illustration of the way in which classical architects worked upon native models. In some points there is an almost servile imitation of the original, and yet the whole tone and feeling are thoroughly non-Egyptian. It does not need a study of the inscriptions to tell us that, though dedicated to Osiris, Isis, and Horus, the sway of those deities had already passed away.

Though the temple at Dakkeh is but little older than that at Dandour, it has an interesting history. Its *adytum* was built by Ergamun, an Ethiopian monarch, who broke through the barbarous customs of his race and set at defiance the tyranny of the priests. Diodorus tells us that up to this time the priests had always informed the king when the time had arrived for him to die, whereupon, in obedience to their commands, he slew himself. This strange custom seems to have grown out of a feeling, like that which prevailed among our Norse ancestors, that it was disgraceful for a warrior to die from disease or old age, and the *sagas* record several instances of aged chiefs rushing on certain death to escape so dishonourable an end. Sir Gardner Wilkinson points out that a similar custom yet exists amongst certain Ethiopian races which lie farther to the south. Ergamun having received the intimation that the time had come to immolate himself, he not only refused to obey, but collecting his troops, marched to the temple, slew the priests, and effected a thorough reform of the whole system. Ergamun clearly distinguished between submission to the priests and reverence for the gods, for he is represented on the walls of the temple as making the accustomed offerings to the deities, and the usual cartouches declare that he was " protected by Amon," " the chosen of Ra," and " the beloved of Isis." [1]

About twenty-five miles above Dakkeh are the remains of a temple belonging to the earliest period, that of Ramses the Great. It is called by the Arabs the Wady Sabooah, the Valley of the Lions, from the avenues of sphinxes which led up to the propylon in front of the temple. At the entrance of the avenue stand two colossal statues of Ramses, with sculptures recording his victories and celebrating his glories. Most of the sphinxes are buried in the sand which has drifted over them, but their huge heads protruding from the plain have a most impressive effect, and fill with awe the wandering Bedouin, who regard them as the work of demons.

Sailing up the river for about seventy miles above Wady Sabooah, through ranges of desert hills, sloping down to green banks, studded with palm and mimosa, or standing cliff-like over the stream, we see before us a bold mass of rock upon which, as we approach it, colossal figures become visible. They are so vast that they look like some freak of nature rather than the work

---

[1] There can be no doubt that in the legend of Ergamenes, which is corroborated by Strabo's account of a similar custom, we have the record of the disappearance of an ancient African custom, by which the reigning king was required to kill himself at the end of a certain term of years, the object being to secure that the king should always be a man in full vigour. Petrie has pointed out that some of the details of the famous " Sed " festival in ancient Egypt, which in historic times came to be merely a kind of royal Jubilee, point to a similar custom having prevailed in Egypt in prehistoric times.

MERFNPTAH, SUCCESSOR TO RAMSES II.

of puny men. It is Abu-Simbel—one of the temples of
the great Ramses and worthy to rank with the edifices
of Thebes or Gîzeh. Elsewhere, the great Egyptian
builders had erected their edifices upon the surface of
the earth. Here a mountain had been hollowed into
shrines for the gods, and hewed into imperishable
monuments of the glory of Pharaoh.

The smaller of the two temples is cut into the rock
to the depth of ninety feet. It was dedicated to Hathor,
the Lady of Aboshek, as she is called. The façade,
ninety feet in length, represents Ramses standing among
the gods, as though their equal in dignity and power.[1]
In the interior, the mild, gentle face of the goddess
appears on the walls amongst her kindred deities, whilst
the hero-king records his conquests of the world as far
as it was then known.

Elsewhere this temple would rivet our attention
upon itself : here it is dwarfed almost into insignificance
by its companion. Four granite warders hewn out of
the living rock keep watch at its portals, seated in solemn
majesty, as they have sat for nearly four thousand years.
Figures fail to convey any adequate sense of their magnitude. As given by Murray, their dimensions are as
follows : " Their total height is about sixty-six feet
without the pedestal ; the ear measures three feet five
inches ; from the inner side of elbow joint to end of
middle finger, fifteen feet. The total height of the
façade of the temple may be between ninety and one
hundred feet." The lower part of the figures is buried
in sand, but they tower so high above the drifted mass,

---

[1] The figures on the façade of the smaller temple of Abu-Simbel
represent, not Ramses among the gods, but Ramses with his wife
Nefertari.

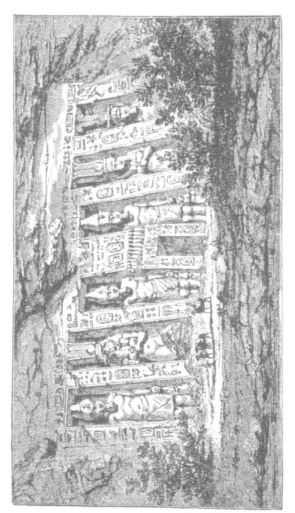

FAÇADE OF SMALLER TEMPLE OF ABU-SIMBEL.

that it is a task of some labour to climb up into the lap of one of them.

The beauty of the faces is even more remarkable than their enormous magnitude. Usually we associate a coarseness and rudeness of finish with great size in works of art : but every visitor is struck by the delicacy and expressiveness of the features. One writer speaks of " the sweet sad smile of the placid pensive face : " another is fascinated by " the expression placid and cheerful—full of moral grace : " a third sees in them a " dignity and composure, a tranquil pity, a serene hopefulness more than human : " a fourth says, " They are unique in art. The masterpieces of Greece, higher in rank, have nothing to match with the mystic beauty of these." There may be some exaggeration in these words. And yet the solemn expressiveness of these colossi cannot be doubted.

The head of one of the statues is broken off, the other three are tolerably perfect. On the leg of one of them is a curious Greek inscription. Herodotus relates that the troops of King Psammetichus who were stationed at Syene, growing weary and mutinous, deserted, and fled into Ethiopia. They were pursued by order of the king. Two of the soldiers who were sent to bring back the fugitives have here recorded the fact, and given their names—Damearchon and Pelephus—as forming part of the expedition. It is seldom that an historical narrative receives such contemporaneous illustration and confirmation. Still more seldom is it that the bad, though ancient, custom of scratching obscure names upon a venerable monument possesses any value whatever.[1]

---

[1] The Greek inscription on the leg of the damaged colossus at Abu Simbel refers, not to the incident referred to in the text, which

The mountain behind these gigantic figures is hollowed out to a depth of about two hundred feet. The excavations consist of a grand hall, with eight side chapels

ETHIOPIAN, NEGRO, AND ASIATIC CAPTIVES BEFORE RAMSES.

opening into it, a second smaller hall, a corridor, and an adytum with altar and figures in relief. The walls are covered with paintings and sculptures, and in the grand

happened in the reign of Psamtek I. (Herodotus II. 30), but to an expedition of Psamtek II., also mentioned by Herodotus (II. 161). The inscription runs as follows. " When King Psammetichus came to Elephantine they wrote this, who came with Psammetichus, son of Theocles, and proceeded by way of Kerkis as far as the river allowed of it. Potasimto led the foreigners, Amasis the Egyptians. Archon, son of Amoibichos, and Pelekos, son of Udamos, wrote this."

hall are eight colossal Osiride columns twenty feet in
height, each standing erect with its back against a square
shaft, thus forming a central aisle.   They are all exactly
alike, with the same placid solemn expression as those
in the façade.   Each is crowned with the serpent-crested
Pshent, and holds in its hands, which are crossed upon

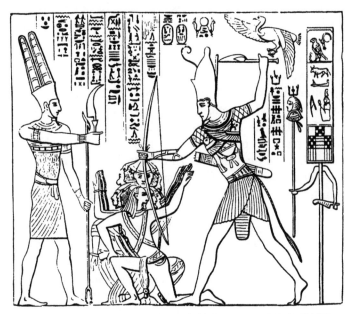

RAMSES SLAYING A GROUP OF AFRICAN AND ASIATIC CAPTIVES

the breast, the crook and flail or scourge, emblems of
divine power and judgment.   They are robed from
head to foot in the close-fitting tunic or shroud of
death.   Round the loins a belt is tied, falling in lappets
upon the knee, and bearing the cartouche of Ramses.

The walls are glowing with colour, like the pages of
an illuminated missal magnified a thousandfold.   Their

theme is everywhere the same—the glory of Ramses. We cannot fail, however, to be struck by the contrast between the tranquil, gentle face of the deified monarch, and the deeds of savage ferocity which are here ascribed to him.   Long lines of captives are led bound before him on their way to execution.   He himself is depicted as slaying them with a pitiless cruelty.   In one sculpture he is grasping by their hair a group of prisoners, representing the various nations, African and Asiatic, which he has conquered.   With his uplifted sword he is about to decapitate them.   The god Amon hands him a scimitar, in token of his approval of the deed.   We follow the mighty conqueror throughout his campaigns. In one place he is charging in his war-chariot upon a whole phalanx of Libyans.   In another, he, single-handed, slays their chief.   In a third he is laying waste the territory of the Ethiopians.   But everywhere his countenance wears the same expression of tranquillity and repose which nothing can disturb.

The entrance to the temple is so small, that only a feeble ray of light can penetrate, leaving the halls in utter darkness, which is imperfectly dispelled by the aid of candles or torches.   But as the opening is towards the east, there are certain seasons of the year at which the light of the rising sun or moon falls full into the vast area.   This of course only happens when the point on the horizon at which the luminary rises exactly fronts the entrance, that is to say, twice in the year with the sun, once a month with the moon.   Then for a few minutes a beam of light streams through the narrow portal, penetrates the great hall, and finds its way into the very adytum, illuminating as with magical effect the figures there.   This innermost shrine was dedicated

GREAT TEMPLE AT ABU-SIMBEL.

to the Sun and Moon, whose symbols are over the altar. We may, therefore, conjecture that the internal arrangements of the temple were originally planned so that on the great festivals this impressive spectacle might be witnessed.

At Abu-Simbel our Egyptian tour terminates. We drift slowly down the Nile, gliding past the ruins of departed greatness. As we revisit the shattered monuments of the most gigantic system of idolatry which the world has ever seen, the contrast between bygone glory and present degradation is forced upon us. It is impossible to forget that, when Egypt was at the summit of its pride and power, its impending doom was again and again foretold by Hebrew prophets. When Thebes was in her glory, and her subsequent conquerors were only wild hordes of the desert, Joel began the warning :—

" Egypt shall be a desolation, and Edom shall be a desolate wilderness,
For the violence against the children of Judah,
Because they have shed innocent blood in their land.
But Judah shall dwell for ever, and Jerusalem from generation to generation." [1]

A hundred years later, Isaiah renewed the burden :—

" The Egyptians will I give over into the hand of a cruel lord ;
And a fierce king shall rule over them, saith the Lord, the Lord of hosts.
Surely the princes of Zoan are fools,
The counsel of the wise counsellors of Pharaoh is become brutish :
How say ye unto Pharaoh, I am the son of the wise, the son of ancient kings ? " [2]

The doom was again denounced by Ezekiel, when the destroyer was nearer at hand, yet still before the long and flourishing reign of Amasis :—

[1] Joel iii. 19, 20.   [2] Isaiah xix. 4, 11.

K

" I am against thee, Pharaoh king of Egypt,
The great dragon that lieth in the midst of his rivers,
Which hath said, My river is mine own, and I have made it for myself.
And all the inhabitants of Egypt shall know that I am the Lord,
Because they have been a staff of reed to the house of Israel.
And the sword shall come upon Egypt, and great pain shall be in
  Ethiopia,
When the slain shall fall in Egypt, and they shall take away her
  multitude,
And her foundations shall be broken down.
And they shall know that I am the Lord,
When I have set fire in Egypt, and when all her helpers shall be
  destroyed.
Thus saith the Lord God : I will also destroy the idols,
And I will cause their images to cease out of Noph ;
And there shall be no more a prince of the land of Egypt :
And I will put a fear in the land of Egypt, and I will make Pathros
  desolate,
And will set fire in Zoan, and will execute judgments in No.
And I will pour My fury upon Sin, the strength of Egypt ;
And I will cut off the multitude of No.
And I will set fire in Egypt : Sin shall have great pain,
And No shall be rent asunder, and Noph shall have distresses daily.
The young men of Aven and of Pi-beseth shall fall by the sword :
And these cities shall go into captivity.
At Tehaphnehes also the day shall be darkened,
When I shall break there the yokes of Egypt :
And the pomp of her strength shall cease in her :
As for her, a cloud shall cover her, and her daughter shall go into
  captivity.
Thus will I execute judgments in Egypt : and they shall know that
  I am the Lord." [1]

Blended with these denunciations of impending ruin
are the promises of a bright and glorious future. As
we trace the exact and literal fulfilment of the one, we
gain new confidence in the full and final accomplishment
of the other. If He " who delighteth in mercy, and
judgment is His strange work," has not allowed one
word of His threatenings to fail, how much more shall
His gracious assurances of pardon and restoration be
verified !

[1] Ezekiel xxix. 3, 6 ; xxx. 4, 8, 13–19.

CHAPTER IV

SOME RESULTS OF MODERN EXCAVATION IN EGYPT

THE closing years of the nineteenth century and the opening ones of the twentieth will probably have few higher claims to the interest of posterity than those constituted by the revelations which they have given to us of the history, the culture, and the art and literature of the great nations of the ancient world. Egypt, Assyria, Babylonia, Persia, have all contributed to our more intimate knowledge of the great classical empires of the ancient East ; while Anatolia has given back to us the relics of the enigmatic Hittite culture, and Mycenæ, Tiryns, and, above all, Knossos, have told us of the brilliancy of that Minoan civilisation which was for so long believed to be only a poet's dream.

Nowhere have the results of the modern passion for investigation been more abundant or striking than in the Land of the Pharaohs, and a book which deals with that land would be fulfilling its object very imperfectly unless it dealt with the discoveries which have added to our knowledge, and discussed their bearing on our conception of the culture of the Egyptian state. The Egypt which Dr. Manning describes with such vivacity in these pages is the Egypt of a time when scientific excavation, as it is now understood, was a thing unknown, and when our material for the study of the genius and accomplishment of the most wonderful race of antiquity was not one tenth of what it is now. When the journey was made whose record is so pleasantly unrolled before us here, Mariette was still at the head of the Egyptian Service of Antiquities—a despotic, even if a benevolent monarch, who would allow no questioning of his royal prerogative, and who granted permission to excavate to no one, not even to his dearest friends, or to men of science of world-wide reputation.

Mariette himself was, no doubt, a miracle of energy, as the thirty-seven sites where he excavated in Egypt testify ; but it was an utter impossibility for any one man, no matter how energetic, to hold the threads of investigation all over Egypt in his hand. He was overwhelmed with work, which in consequence was never quite thoroughly done ; and many competent workers were held back from service which they were eager to render, while the prohibition which hindered them had no effect on the native Egyptian practitioner of the art of excavation, a tomb-robber by nature and descent, who followed as diligently as ever his ancestors' practice of robbing the great dead of past ages and disposing of their treasures to the curio-hunting tourist, save when he was occupied in the fabrication of modern antiques to meet the demand.

With Mariette's death (January 18, 1881), however, the modern period may be definitely said to begin ; and it is from that year that we shall take up the tale of discovery. The late Sir Gaston Maspero, who succeeded the first Director, began his reign with the record of one of those big spectacular discoveries, which, if they do not always do so much for our actual increase of

THE TEMPLE OF LUXOR.

knowledge as some less noticeable ones, have at least this advantage that they catch the public imagination, and result in increase of that material support without which excavation cannot be carried on.

For several years, in fact since 1873, it had been becoming apparent that the fellahs had somehow got access to some rich store of royal funerary furniture ; for papyri, chiefly of XXIst Dynasty period, were being quietly put on the market.

Suspicion gradually gathered round one family, the Abd er-Rasuls of Kurna, and in April, 1881, Maspero arrested Ahmed, one of the family, and committed him for examination to the tender mercies of the Mudir of Keneh, Daoud Pasha, whose methods of administering justice and extracting information were both picturesque and drastic. Daoud's examination, conducted with what Maspero diplomatically calls " his customary severity," produced nothing but protestations of spotless innocence, and the virtuous Ahmed had to be provisionally released ; but, as Mr. Howard Carter puts it, " His interview with Daoud seems to have shaken him. Interviews with Daoud usually did have that effect."

After some weeks of bitter family quarrels and recriminations, another member of the Abd er-Rasul family, Mohammed, came to the dreaded Mudir, and made as complete a confession as was convenient, though the manner in which he and his brothers made their discovery was never disclosed. The chief point of his confession was his promise to guide an official of the Service of Antiquities to the scene of the family gold-mine ; and on July 5th, 1881, he led Emil Brugsch and Ahmed Effendi Kemal of the Service to a lonely spot not far from Hatshepsut's temple at Der el-Bahri.

Brugsch was lowered down the black shaft of the
unfinished tomb of Astemkheb, one of the queens of
the XXIst Dynasty, and forty feet below the surface
he found a long gallery ending in a chamber, both gallery
and chamber packed with the remains of dead Pharaohs.
It seemed as though almost all the most famous monarchs
of the great days of the Empire had been gathered
together, with their queens, in this lonely and desolate
spot, to await their resurrection ; and indeed this was
not far from being the case.   There were Thothmes II.
and his greater successor Thothmes III., the greatest
of Egypt's soldiers ; there was the earlier champion,
Seqenen-Ra, who began the long struggle which ended
in the expulsion of the Hyksos ; there were Sety I. and
Ramses II., the most famous monarchs of the
XIXth Dynasty, and Ramses III., of the XXth Dynasty,
the last great warrior king of Egypt ; there were
Pinezem I. and Pinezem II. of the XXIst Dynasty ;
and along with the kings were found some of the most
famous Egyptian queens, Aahmes Nefertari and
Aahhotep, of the XVIIIth, Hent-taui, Nezem-mut, and
Astemkheb of the XXIst Dynasty.   Altogether this
amazing haul of royal and princely personages embraced
something like forty mummies with a considerable amount
of funerary furniture, though not so much as might have
been expected.

Bewildered as he must have been by the unparalleled
richness of the find, Brugsch at once took steps to have
his treasures placed in security.   Three hundred Arabs,
of Kurna, " each one a thief " as Brugsch says, and
each, no doubt bitterly resenting the interference which
was going to deprive him of a fertile source of income,
were at once employed to hoist up and pack the mummies,

HEAD OF QUEEN NEFERTARI, WIFE OF RAMSES II.
(*From a sculpture at Abu-Simbel.*)

and after six days of hard labour (a curious contrast to the care and deliberation which have marked the handling of the treasures of Tutankhamen's tomb), the whole of the treasures of the Der el-Bahri *cache* were ready for the Museum steamboat which was to transport them to Cairo. The steamer was accompanied on her voyage by frantic crowds of men and women, wailing, cursing, and firing rifles ; and the mummies were finally safely lodged in the Cairo Museum to await unwrapping.

The final unwrapping was delayed till 1886, owing to a catastrophe which occurred when the first attempt took place. It was accomplished in the spring and early summer of that year, and the faces of the most famous or best preserved of these ancient monarchs are now as familiar to the general public as those of any modern monarchs—on the whole a somewhat pitiful spectacle, and one whose extension is not to be encouraged. The wrappings frequently bore dockets which proved that their assemblage in the pit of Der el-Bahri was due to the anxiety of the priests of the XXIst Dynasty, who found it impossible any longer to protect the scattered and lonely tombs under their charge from the attacks of the professional tomb-robbers, who then, as now, abounded in the neighbourhood of Thebes. Several of the mummies had been buried again and again in the vain effort to find security ; but the black-shaft at Der el-Bahri had kept its secret well for three thousand years.

From this astounding haul of buried royalties dates the modern period of interest in the study of ancient Egypt, its monuments, and above all, its tombs. On the whole, it was chiefly from the Biblical side that the thing appealed to the public. That it should be possible, as seemed to be the case, that you could look upon

the actual face of the king who made the lives of the
Israelites bitter with hard service in brick and mortar,
and from whose anger Moses fled into the land of Midian
—this seemed to very many the height of the romance of
history. A great impulse was immediately given to
Egyptology, and it is from this time that almost all
the great exploration societies of the various nations
date. The Egypt Exploration Society was founded in
1883, and was speedily followed by French, German,
and American Societies of a similar nature, and excavation work began in Egypt on a scale never before
attempted.

Fortunately for the future of the work, the creation
of this great new opportunity roughly coincided with
the rise into recognition of the merits of the great
excavator who by his insistence on " the importance of
' unconsidered trifles,' " as Dr. Macalister puts it, has
done more than any other man to create the science of
modern excavation—Professor Sir W. M. Flinders
Petrie. His energies were at once enlisted in the service
of the new Society, and in 1884 he began to excavate
at Tanis, the Biblical Zoan, and the Delta capital of the
Hyksos usurpers. Some work had already been done
here by the indefatigable Mariette ; but the whole site
was now surveyed and cleared as far as possible.
Abundant evidence came to light of the importance of
the town in all periods of Egyptian history ; but perhaps
the most remarkable single find was that of the remains
of the huge standing statue of Ramses II. in red granite.
The colossus had been broken into fragments ; but
enough of one foot remained for the size of the whole
figure to be calculated. From the top of his crown to
the base of his pedestal, Ramses stood 92 feet in height,

and with the built-up pedestal beneath the block the whole must have reached a height of 125 feet. It was thus by far the tallest single figure ever erected by the Egyptians, the great colossus of the Ramesseum measuring only 57⅓ feet. The latter figure, however, was a sitting one, and the two great blocks probably weighed much the same, about 1000 tons !

Meanwhile M. Edouard Naville had also been excavating for the Society at Tell el-Maskhuteh, and had found there what seemed conclusive evidence of the identity of the place with the " store-city Pithom " which the Israelites are recorded to have built, with its companion Raamses, for the Pharaoh of the Oppression. This identification, long accepted, has, however, been questioned of late days by Gardiner and others, and the matter is still in dispute.

The season of 1885 brought another remarkable identification, for Petrie found, at Nebireh, unmistakable evidence that this was the site of the famous Greek colony of Naukratis, one of the two great garrison-cities in which Psamtek I. settled his Greek mercenaries, the " brazen men from the sea," whose valour and discipline had secured for him the crown of Egypt. Abundant evidence of the Greek occupation was found, in the shape of Greek pottery and relics of the Pan-Hellenion, and temples to Aphrodite and Apollo. In 1886 the companion site, that of the camp of Daphnæ, was found at a spot called Tell Def'neh, on the eastern side of the Delta. Here were traced the remains of a great fortified camp, which bears the local name, Kasr Bint el Yehudi ; " The Palace of the Jew's Daughter," a title which at once brings to mind the passage (Jer. xliii. 5–13), which describes how after the fall of Jerusalem, Johanan the

son of Kareah " took all the remnant of Judah . . . and
the king's daughters . . . and Jeremiah the prophet. . . .
So they came into the land of Egypt . . . Thus came
they even to Tahpanhes." There can be little
doubt that the camp of Daphnæ is the spot to which
Jeremiah refers, and that the local name " Kasr Bint
el-Yehudi," even if, as Professor Peet suggests, it " may
well have originated in much later times," preserves a
true tradition of the spot where the Jewish exile princesses
found a brief refuge before the blast of Nebuchadnezzar's
invasion drove them further south again.

Further important work was done in the Delta by
Naville, who in 1887-1889 excavated the site of Bubastis,
the capital of the Libyan Pharaohs, the Sheshanks and
Osorkons of the XXIInd Dynasty, revealing the remains
of the great festival hall of Osorkon II., and many relics
of earlier periods, including the base of a great statue of
Khyan, the most famous of the Hyksos kings, traces of
whom are found in quarters as widely separated as
Knossos, in Crete, and Baghdad.

Meanwhile Petrie had been working at Hawara,
near the mouth of the Fayum, where he accumulated
much valuable evidence as to the work of the great kings
of the Middle Kingdom, and especially that of
Amenemhat III., whose pyramid lies here. But the
most valuable result of his excavations at this spot was
the discovery, in a cemetery mostly dating from the first
and second centuries of our era, of a large number of
funerary portraits painted in coloured wax. In 1911
further additions were made to this gathering of the
only relics of ancient art in the shape of panel pictures
which have survived to tell us of the manner in which
the great Greek masterpieces of Apelles, Polygnotus,

Panainos, and their fellow-workers may have been wrought. The Hawara portraits, of course, are far from being masterpieces, being merely the work of the local firms of undertakers; their importance consists in the evidence which they afford as to the materials used and the technique employed in ancient painting. The first great collection of Greco-Roman papyri was also the fruit of Petrie's work at Hawara, which thus prepared the way for a branch of Egyptology which has had such enormous developments within the last twenty-five years.

At Illahun in 1889–1890 the same unwearying worker gave us the complete plan of the XIIth Dynasty town of Kahun, which had housed the workmen employed in the building of the pyramid of Senusert II., and thus enabled us to realise something of the condition of the Egyptian workman of 4000 years ago; while in 1891 his excavations at the pyramid of Seneferu at Medum revealed the earliest extant specimen of an Egyptian temple—the little pyramid temple which crouched at the base of the pyramid, and in which offerings were made to and for Seneferu.

The same year witnessed the beginning of Petrie's work at Tell el-Amarna, where the palace of Akhenaten, with its wonderful painted pavements and its gorgeous decorative work in coloured glazes, was revealed. Since then the work at the heretic capital has been carried on by the German Expedition, whose discoveries of the sculpture of the period have been of the utmost value in the study of the new development of realistic art which characterised the Aten supremacy; while the British expedition has since the war carried the work still further, and disclosed the workmen's town, where the craftsmen who created the faience and glaze industries of el-Amarna lived.

In 1894–1895 came de Morgan's wonderful treasure-trove at Dahshur, when the discovery of the jewelled diadems, pectorals, and bracelets of Khnumit and other XIIth Dynasty princesses gave to the world a new conception of the skill of the Egyptian goldsmith of the Middle Kingdom, alike in design and execution. Nothing finer than the two diadems of Khnumit with their exquisite floral and conventional designs and their delicate cloison setting of precious and semi-precious stones, has ever been found ; and it is hard to believe that even the treasures of Tutankhamen's tomb, marvellous as they may be, can surpass these astonishing specimens of XIIth Dynasty craftsmanship.

In 1895 and the subsequent years till 1898, attention was drawn to Abydos, the Holy City of the Egyptian faith, and the burial place of the head of Osiris, by the excavations carried on there by the French Mission under M. Amélineau. The results were sufficiently startling, for in 1898 Amélineau announced his discovery of the actual tomb and bier of the God of the Resurrection himself, while part of a skull found in the tomb was conjectured to be the actual head of Osiris. The somewhat headlong and slovenly methods of the French explorer, however, and the bitter controversy which ensued upon his proclamation of his finds, and resulted in the demonstration that the so-called Bed of Osiris was a restoration of the New Empire, rather cast discredit upon the claims of Abydos, and the place was left for a little, until more patient and skilful methods in the hands of an explorer who was better equipped for such a task gave back to the Holy City its pride of place, and revealed to the world a whole chapter of Egyptian history which for long had been believed to belong only to the realm of myth.

One of the things for which Egyptologists, and Bible students in particular, had been longing, was some Egyptian record mentioning that Hebrew race, whose fortunes were so long and so intimately linked with those of the empire of the Nile ; and it was hoped and believed that the discovery of such a mention would clear up much that was obscure. In 1896 the long-looked for discovery came. In that year, Petrie, who was working among the funerary temples of the kings of the XVIIIth and XIXth Dynasties on the west bank of the Nile at Thebes, found among the ruins of the temple of Merenptah the son and successor of that Ramses II. who was believed to be the Pharaoh of the Oppression, and who therefore should be himself the Pharaoh of the Exodus, a black granite stele of Amenhotep III., which had been appropriated, along with much else of the same king's work, by Merenptah. Its original front bore an inscription of Amenhotep ; but on the back Merenptah had engraved a long song of triumph in which all his victories over the enemies of Egypt were recorded. In the midst of this song comes the reference to Israel so much desired. The passage runs as follows :

" Plundered is the Canaan, with every evil,
Carried off is Askelon,
Seized upon is Gezer,
Yenoam is made as a thing that is not.
Israel is desolated, her seed is not,
Palestine has become as a defenceless widow for Egypt."

The immediate result of such an unexpected form of reference was, obviously, not to help the situation, but to make confusion worse confounded. If Merenptah, as seemed almost certain to the opinion of the time, were the Pharaoh of the Exodus, how did it come about that he could record a victory over the Israelites, who are manifestly, from the setting of the reference, contemplated as being already settled in Palestine ?   Theories of all sorts, involving all kinds of expedients to meet the awkward situation, were plentiful for several years, and then opinion, fortified by what seemed the clear reference to the invading Hebrew tribes in the Tell el-Amarna Tablets, which had been found by hazard by a fellah woman among the ruins of Akhenaten's palace in 1887, and were now manifesting their importance as sources for the history of the period from 1400 to 1350 B.C., showed signs of definitely swaying round to a date for the Exodus about two centuries earlier than that which had previously been accepted. The invading Habiri of the Tell el-Amarna Letters, it was argued, could scarcely be anything else, especially in the light of the Merenptah stele, than the Tribes under Joshua, making their first inroads on the land which Merenptah found them holding two centuries later. The date for the Exodus, therefore, was provisionally fixed in the reign of Amenhotep II., roughly about 1430 B.C. For the last twenty years or so this view has steadily been attracting to itself the weight of skilled opinion, and has been growing to an accepted fact, though there have always been some who have refused to accept it.

Now, however, the wheel appears to be making another revolution, and recent discoveries in Palestine seem to indicate that perhaps the Ramses and Merenptah date may be the truth after all, in which case another explanation of the Merenptah stele will have to be found. It

may be remarked in passing that the hero of the hour in
excavation, Tutankhamen, has been pressed, as was to
be expected, into the service, and it has been gravely
asserted that he is the only real, true, and original Pharaoh
of the Exodus—an opinion which seems to combine all
the disadvantages of all the other views, and none of their
advantages. Manifestly nothing but new and positive
facts can settle this long-vexed question, and until these
shall be forthcoming speculation is merely vanity and
a striving after wind.

In 1898 the scene of interest shifted again to the
Valley of the Kings at Thebes, and M. Loret, acting
upon information gathered locally, opened up several
royal tombs. Of these the most interesting proved
to be that of Amenhotep II. (1448–1420 B.C.), the son
and successor of the great conqueror Thothmes III.
Here the priests of the XXIst Dynasty, despairing of
being able to protect the scattered tombs of the kings,
had gathered no fewer than thirteen royal mummies,
among them that of Merenptah, the supposed Pharaoh
of the Exodus. But the chief interest of the discovery
lay in the fact that for the first time the mummy of a
Pharaoh was now found lying in the sarcophagus where
it had been laid more than 3000 years before. With
Amenhotep II. in his great carved stone sarcophagus
under the blue-painted, gold-starred roof, lay his famous
bow of which he boasted that " no one could draw it
among his army, among the hill-country sheikhs, or
among the princes of the Retenu, because his strength
is so much greater than that of any king who has ever
existed." An inscription on it read : " Smiter of the
Cave-dwellers, overthrower of the Kush, hacking up
their cities . . . the great wall of Egypt, protector of

his soldiers." Besides the king himself, and Merenptah, there were found in the tomb the mummies of Thothmes IV., Amenhotep III., Siphtah, Ramses IV., Ramses V., and Ramses VI., together with other princely personages. The tomb had already been plundered in ancient times, so that little of artistic value was found ; but several articles of funerary furniture still remained. In this case the experiment was tried of leaving the great king to rest in his coffin along with some of his funerary equipment ; but shortly after the discovery the tomb was broken into by armed robbers, the mummy of Amenhotep tumbled out upon the floor, and the model of a funerary boat stolen. Arrests were made ; but it proved impossible to secure a conviction, nor has the boat ever been recovered. Amenhotep was restored to his sarcophagus, and has since been allowed to rest in peace, save for the visits of tourists, who are treated to the spectacle of the face of the dead king theatrically lighted up by electric light ; but the incident warns us of the danger which undoubtedly attends the proposal to allow the body of Tutankhamen, should it be found within the great crystalline sandstone sarcophagus under the gilded canopy, to remain where it was laid nearly 3300 years ago. In theory, and sentimentally, the proposal is most attractive ; but there can be no doubt that practically it is attended with great danger. Every fellah in the district will be firmly persuaded that wealth, "beyond the dreams of avarice," lies beside the dead king, and will consider that the treasures of the tomb are his natural and rightful prey ; and very careful guarding both of the tomb and of the guards will be necessary if Tutankhamen is not to suffer the same fate which befell Amenhotep.

OUTER MUMMY CASE OF QUEEN NEFERTARI.

In the winter of 1899 Professor Petrie was at length allowed to resume at Abydos the work which had been abandoned by Amélineau. The result of his labours was a very remarkable addition to our knowledge of the history and the culture of the earliest Dynastic period. Previously the history of Egypt before the time of the Pyramid-builders of the IVth Dynasty had been simply a matter of vague legend, in which shadowy kings, with incredible stories attached to them, loomed dimly through the mists of the past. Petrie's work gave back to us the solid realities which lay behind the old legends of Manetho. The tombs of the early Dynastic monarchs conformed, in the main, to a single type—that of a square or oblong subterranean chamber, sometimes lined with wood, sometimes floored with stone, and sometimes, as in the case of the tomb of Khasekhemui of the IInd Dynasty, completely built of stone—the earliest example of masonry in the world. Around the central chamber, where doubtless the body of the dead king was laid, were grouped smaller chambers, which had once contained the funerary furniture and the provision for the needs of the king in his journey through the Underworld, and also the bodies of those of his favourites who had been slain to be his companions in the realm of the dead.

Nothing, of course, was found intact. The tombs had been rifled at a very early date, and in several cases bore the marks of fire,—these earliest of tomb-robbers dealing with their prey as the Ramesside plunderers did with the body of King Sebek-em-saf. No royal bodies were found, and the only directly personal relic was the arm of the queen of King Zer, which had been thrust by some robber, no doubt disturbed in his nefarious

L

task, into a hole in the wall, where it was found by one
of Petrie's workmen. It still bore four bracelets of gold,
turquoise, and amethyst, which provide the evidence
that the Egyptian goldsmith of the earliest period was
already a finished craftsman, whose work, alike in design
and execution, is worthy of comparison with the best
work of later days. In other respects the fragments
left in the tomb were simply what the robbers of early
days had not deemed worth the trouble of carrying away,
ivory and ebony labels, inscribed with hieroglyphs,
archaic in form, but quite intelligible, broken pieces of
ivory furniture, and vessels of pottery and hard stone,
in the working of which the Egyptian workman of
6000 years ago had attained an astonishing proficiency.
But, fragmentary as the relics of the Royal Tombs of
Abydos may be, they have furnished the evidence that
the Egyptian state of the earliest dynasties was already
far removed from barbarism. Six thousand years ago
great kings, Narmer, Aha-men, " The Scorpion," Den,
Zer, and others like them, ruled over an Egypt already
united, " Lords of the Two Lands," commanded great
armies, whose movements swept into the power of the
conquering Pharaoh huge masses of prisoners (120,000
men in one inscription of King Narmer), moved in the
midst of a court as well and completely organised as that
of any modern kingdom, and were housed in a palace
where comfort and artistic taste were ministered to by
furniture and decoration of fine design and material,
wrought with a high degree of technical skill. The
relics of the earliest dynastic period from Abydos appear,
it may be, comparatively insignificant beside the richer
finds of later periods ; but their actual importance is of
the very highest, for they have restored to us several

centuries of human history, and have made the earliest
Egypt a reality instead of a shadow.

The work at Abydos has since been carried on by
Naville, Peet, and Hall, with results of remarkable
interest. Perhaps the most striking feature of the later
work has been the discovery, behind the great temple of
Sety I., of the underground building, with great monolith
pillars of granite, and a series of small chambers surrounding a central block, which may perhaps have been
separated by a tank of water from the rest of the building,
though this is not certain. This building is doubtless
the true Osireion, and should the idea of the tank prove
to be well-grounded, we should probably see here the
" well " to which Strabo refers.[1] Part of this building is
of New Empire date, and bears inscriptions of
Merenptah ; but the central part, with the huge mono-
lithic pillars (far larger than those of the so-called
" Temple of the Sphinx "), is not improbably contemporary with the work of the Pyramid-builders.

In 1902, Mr. T. M. Davis, a wealthy American,
was granted the right to excavate in the Valley of
the Kings under the supervision of the Service of
Antiquities, and for the next six years the excavations,
for which he provided the funds, while the actual work
was carried out by Messrs. Quibell, Weigall, Howard
Carter, and the late Mr. Ayrton, were crowned with
the most astonishing success. In 1902, Mr. Carter
found the tomb of Thothmes IV. of the XVIIIth Dynasty.
The mummy of this king was one of those found in 1898
in the tomb of Amenhotep II., and the tomb had been

---

[1] Professor Petrie is of opinion that the underground building
never was a pool, but that the so-called water space is merely the
gap left where limestone has been stripped out, to be used for other
building purposes.

already rifled, and most of the relics remaining in it had
been smashed by the robbers ; but a great deal of interesting material was gathered, perhaps the finest piece being
the front of the king's chariot, adorned with reliefs of
battle wrought in gesso.

Next year the same explorer found the royal tomb of
one of the most interesting figures of Egyptian history—
Queen Hatshepsut.   The resting-place which this master-
ful lady had provided for herself is one of the largest of
the royal tombs, measuring over 700 feet in length,
and 100 in vertical depth ; but it was never finished,
and is without inscriptions or reliefs.   Moreover it had
been most thoroughly plundered, and scarcely anything
was left to reward the modern excavators, save the two
sarcophagi of red crystalline sandstone, one for Hatshepsut
herself, the other for her father Thothmes I.   It may be
conjectured that Hatshepsut had the sarcophagus of
her father removed to her own tomb.   Subsequently,
in the scramble for safety during the XXIst Dynasty
the mummy of Thothmes was removed to the *cache* at
Der el-Bahri, where it was found in 1881 ; and possibly
one of the unidentified female mummies found at the
same time was that of the great queen.

This discovery, or rather re-discovery, of Hatshepsut's
tomb had a curious sequel.   In 1916 Mr. Howard Carter,
while on holiday at Luxor, was informed that a tomb
had been found on the western side of the mountain
above the Valley of the Kings, and that it had been taken
possession of by armed robbers, who had driven off the
original discoverers.   Mr. Carter, on the invitation of
the local notables, proceeded to the spot, with the few
workmen whom he could gather, and after being lowered
for 130 feet down the face of a sheer cliff came upon

the robbers ensconced in the tomb, and busily at work
by the moonlight. After a somewhat dramatic and
tense negotiation, he remained in possession, and the
robbers scrambled up to the top of the cliff by the rope
which had brought Mr. Carter down. The tomb,
thus strangely recovered, proved to be another tomb of
Queen Hatshepsut, which she had made for herself in
the days when she was only wife of Thothmes II. Later,
when she held the sceptre alone, she had abandoned
this tomb, and hewn out the larger and more pretentious
one in the Valley. As a question of security, probably
the change was a mistake ; for her second tomb had, as
we have seen, been thoroughly rifled. The cliff tomb
on the other hand, was in a very remarkable situation,
130 feet below the top of the cliff, and 220 feet above
the Valley, and so well hidden that neither from above
nor below could a trace of it be seen. Perhaps if the
great queen had been content with this first tomb, she
might have been left in peace to the present day, instead
of being hustled from tomb to tomb, and left at last as
possibly an unidentified mummy among a batch of
Pharaohs. The cliff tomb had never been finished or
occupied, and the only thing which it contained was a
fine unfinished sarcophagus of crystalline sandstone,
which has now with great difficulty been brought down
from its lofty perch, the labour and difficulty of the
operation being such as to increase considerably our
opinion of the skill of the Pharaonic engineers who
hoisted it originally into its position.

Early in 1905 came another important discovery.
It was not that of a Pharaoh, but of two princely person-
ages who are of more interest to us than many of the
Pharaohs, Prince Yuaa and his wife Tuau, the father and

mother of that famous Queen Tiy, who, as the wife of Amenhotep III., and the mother of Akhenaten, exercised perhaps more influence upon the course of history in the Near East during one of its greatest crises than any other single individual. The tomb of Yuaa and Tuau was of entirely undistinguished appearance, but its contents had scarcely been disturbed, and constituted the richest find of ancient Egyptian furniture and works of art which had ever been discovered up to that time. In fact the only find which has excelled this in richness is that of the tomb of Tutankhamen. The mummies of Yuaa and Tuau were wonderfully well preserved, and are now in the Museum of Cairo. Among the chief objects of interest found were several inlaid coffers of fine design, bearing the cartouches of Amenhotep III. and his wife Tiy, the chariot of Yuaa, and the shrine holding the canopic jars which contained the viscera of the dead. The chairs, and the couches, beautifully designed and constructed with the most workmanlike skill, gave a foretaste of the still more remarkable examples of Egyptian craftsmanship which were to be revealed to the world in the tomb of Tutankhamen.

The good fortune of Mr. Davis did not end with the discovery of the tomb of Yuaa. In the winter of 1905, he and the late Mr. E. R. Ayrton discovered the tomb of the Pharaoh Siphtah, of the XIXth Dynasty. It had been thoroughly plundered, and the excavation had to be abandoned at one point owing to the fact that the roof of the chamber had fallen in, rendering work dangerous ; but some of the mural decoration was of high quality, and has been admirably reproduced in the volume devoted to this discovery.

January of 1907 brought a far more interesting find.

Near the tomb of Ramses I. Mr. Davis and Mr. Weigall discovered a vault, for it can scarcely be described as a real tomb, in the entrance to which they found part of a funeral canopy of gilded wood bearing an inscription which stated that Akhenaten made it for his mother, Queen Tiy. Within the vault the explorers found a coffin which had fallen or been thrown down from its supports, and had burst open, disclosing a mummy, or rather the half-decayed bones of a body, which had been crowned with the golden vulture of Egypt, and wrapped in thin sheets of flexible gold. The inscription on the coffin, worked in semi-precious stones, gave the title of Akhenaten, " the beautiful child of the Sun." Along with the coffin, there were found four beautiful canopic jars of alabaster, which, instead of being capped, as usual, with the heads of the " Children of Horus," bore four portrait busts of most exquisite execution. The type of head represented is a very striking one. The inscriptions on the jars had been carefully erased, so that there was no evidence to show to whom the jars belonged ; but Mr. Davis, attracted by the inscription on the canopy, assumed that the jars belonged to Queen Tiy, and that the portrait on the jars was that of the great queen, and the body in the coffin hers also. On examination, however, Professor Elliot Smith pronounced the bones to be those of a young man, of probably not more than twenty-five or twenty-six years of age, though certain abnormal indications suggest the possibility of a somewhat greater age. Finally it became plain, greatly to the disgust of Mr. Davis, who had set his heart on discovering the body of Queen Tiy, that the coffin and the mummy were indeed those of her son Akhenaten, buried in the tomb of his mother in haste and secrecy

after the return of the court from Tell el-Amarna to
Thebes. The probability is that the four beautiful
canopic heads are also portraits of Akhenaten, as
indeed the erasure of the name would suggest. The
type of face represented is strikingly like that of several
of the heads of Akhenaten discovered by the German
expedition at Tell el-Amarna, and now in the Berlin
Museum, and though it may be pleaded that they
resemble also certain portraits of Queen Tiy, it is only
natural to suppose that mother and son had a family
likeness to one another; and while the reason for the
erasure of the inscription is plain if the jars are those of
Akhenaten, there is absolutely no reason for it if they are
those of his mother.

In 1908 Mr. Davis and Mr. Ayrton made the last
discovery of importance which was to reward their
efforts. This was the tomb of Horemheb, the usurping
reactionary soldier who seized the throne after the
ephemeral reign of " The Divine Father Ay," who
succeeded Tutankhamen. Horemheb, like Queen
Hatshepsut, had had another tomb, in this case at
Memphis, in the days when kingship seemed a remote
thing; but when he seized the throne he evidently
determined to be buried like a king in the Valley. Like
Hatshepsut also, he paid the price of his pride, for his
tomb had been plundered and wrecked with the utmost
thoroughness. His red granite sarcophagus, 8 feet
11 inches in length, by 3 feet 9½ inches in breadth,
and 4 feet in depth, was a very fine piece of decorative
carving, and its motives of protecting goddess figures,
shadowing the coffin with their outstretched wings,
seem to be the same as those of the sarcophagus of
Tutankhamen, so far as this has been described. This

succeess closed the record of a most remarkable piece of work, for though the concession was held till 1914, Mr. Davis won no further laurels in the Valley, and indeed, did little more work there, being convinced that, as he expressed it in the introduction to *The Tombs of Harmhabi and Touatankhamanou*, " The Valley of the Tombs is now exhausted." Fortunately for Egyptology this has not proved to be the case ; but fourteen years of interruption due to the war, and of unrewarded effort after the war, were to elapse before the Valley yielded up its next great secret.

The tracing of the footsteps of Mr. Davis in the Valley of the Kings has carried us a little out of the line of events generally ; but the years of his work were by no means unfruitful in other departments of Egyptology. We have already seen that the first great discovery of Greco-Roman papyri was due to Petrie in 1888. It was followed up by the discovery of the wonderful richness of Oxyrhynchus in documents of the Greco-Roman period. The Oxyrhynchus Papyri have proved of the utmost value as first-hand sources of information with regard to life in the Egypt of this period ; while the discovery of certain of the sayings of Jesus unrecorded in the Gospels—the " Logia,"—has given us the nearest approach to what many earnest Biblical students craved as the result of excavation in Palestine—some addition to our knowledge of the words of Him who " spake as never man spake." In 1905 and the following years came the discovery at Elephantine of a remarkable series of Aramaic papyri giving us a great deal of information as to the life of the Jewish community in this furthest corner of Egypt. Indeed the department of papyrus-hunting has now grown to such dimensions as

to have a special literature of considerable extent of
its own.

In the year 1893, Naville began for the Egypt Exploration Fund the huge task of excavating the famous terraced
temple of Queen Hatshepsut at Der el-Bahri. Here
Mariette had done some work already, and had revealed
one of the most interesting of the sculptured scenes of
the temple, the series of reliefs depicting the Voyage to
Punt, and the return of the ships ; but a vast deal
remained to be done in order to make the plan of the
building completely comprehensible, and to secure the
safety of the precious sculptures.

The work of excavation and preservation went on
till the end of the century, and the final volume embodying
the results of the gigantic piece of work was not issued
till 1908. The result of fifteen years of toil was to present to the world a practically complete picture of one
of the most interesting of Egyptian temples—a building
which was for long held to be unique. Subsequent
excavation at Der el-Bahri, however, has proved that
this is not the case.

In 1903, before the final results of the earlier excavation had been published, M. Naville began a new piece
of work among the mounds to the south of Hatshepsut's
temple, in the expectation that an XIth Dynasty cemetery
might lie beneath them ; but the excavations had not
progressed far before the explorers came upon a platform,
obviously a part of another terraced temple, something
like that of Queen Hatshepsut, but of considerably earlier
date. As the work progressed, it became manifest that
the new temple was the funerary chapel of one of the
Pharaohs of the XIth Dynasty, Mentuhotep Neb-hepet-ra,
and that to its architect, who may have been that Mertisen

who has left us from this period an inscription in which he describes his skill as an artist, belongs the credit of having invented that form of terraced temple, rising by successive stages to the level of the sanctuary, which Senmut, Hatshepsut's architect, afterwards used with such triumphant success.

The Mentuhotep temple rises by means of a steep ramp to the first platform, which is faced with a colonnade of pillars, square on plan. From its upper surface rises another colonnade of square pillars supporting a roof, and making a kind of verandah which completely surrounds the central mass of the building. This consists of a hypostyle hall almost square, whose roof is supported by a forest of octagonal pillars. In the centre of this hall rose a rectangular mass of masonry, faced with hewn stone, and capped originally with a small pyramid. This remarkable building had suffered sadly at the hands of the succeeding generations, and had evidently been used as a quarry for material, for nothing was left standing above a height of 10 feet ; but it proved perfectly possible to reconstruct it in imagination as it must have been in the days when it was complete. It is one of the most interesting structures in Egypt—the link between the pyramids with their attached chapels, and the New Empire custom of separating tomb and temple altogether. The XIth Dynasty temple is by no means so imposing or so beautiful a piece of work as its successor of the XVIIIth Dynasty. If Senmut borrowed from the earlier architect, he had that touch of genius which legitimises such borrowings, and transfigures them ; but the older building is superior to its rival in the workmanship which has been put into it, if it be inferior in its plan. The masonry of Hatshepsut's shrine is good enough, according to the standard of its period ; but it cannot be compared to the splendid work of the XIth Dynasty.

Among the finds which the excavation revealed were the shrines of several priestesses, which had been intruded into the fabric after its completion—a fact which has suggested that these ladies were the favourites of the dead king, killed at his death and buried beside him in order that they might accompany him in the Underworld. If this be the case, then these shrines are the latest evidence of this ancient custom, which was soon superseded in the merciful Egyptian mind by the adoption of the " ushabti " custom ; but the evidence is scarcely sufficient to sustain the weight of the theory which has been built upon it.[1]

Several important pieces of Egyptian sculpture came to light in the course of the excavations, among them six magnificent statues in grey granite of Senusert III. of the XIIth Dynasty, one of the greatest kings of Egyptian history, and probably the true Sesostris of Greek legend. In the best preserved of these, the strong truculent features of the great soldier are represented with a power which increases our admiration for the sculptors of the Middle Kingdom who were capable of such powerful characterisation. In a little Hathor shrine which Thothmes III. had intruded into the north corner of the temple, was found in February, 1906, one of the most admirable specimens of Egyptian animal sculpture which has yet come to light—the famous Hathor-cow of Der el-Bahri. Egypt's reputation for such work might safely be staked on this magnificent piece of sculpture, and the two granite lions from Nubia, bearing the names

[1] Professor Petrie and Mr. Winlock hold that the shrines are of earlier construction than is suggested in the text.

of Amenhotep III. and Tutankhamen, which are now in the British Museum.

Meanwhile at Karnak M. Legrain had been carrying on for the Service of Antiquities a piece of work, gigantic in scale, which, though it can scarcely be called excavation, was yet of the utmost importance for the preservation of the greatest monument of Upper Egypt, and resulted incidentally in the discovery of a perfect treasure of Egyptian art. His work was necessitated by the fact that the Pharaonic architects, though in some respects the greatest builders that the world has known, were also in others almost culpably careless. They reared their vast structures on foundations which to our minds seem totally inadequate to the task assigned to them, and the consequence has been that in spite of the mass of the great temples, which in a measure has proved their security, earth tremors and the infiltration of Nile water have wrought havoc in the course of the centuries. For several years it had been manifest that parts of the great temple were becoming insecure, and on October 3rd, 1899, eleven of the columns of the famous Hypostyle Hall fell, while five more showed signs of speedily following their example. This disaster was quickly followed by the partial collapse of the great pylon which bounds the Hall on the west. For awhile it seemed as if the glories of Karnak were doomed to swift destruction. Immediate and strenuous measures were necessary to prevent the destruction from spreading further, and to repair the damage which had already been done, and the work was entrusted to M. Legrain. In carrying out this tremendous task, he gave a curious demonstration of the simplicity of the methods with which the great builders of ancient Egypt wrought their stupendous

works, for he found it both simpler and more economical
to rebuild Karnak by the use of the ramp, the lever, and
the derrick, than to import costly machinery from
Europe to lift and place the huge blocks. For several
years the temple was cumbered with the same style of
earthen ramps which helped the architects of
Thothmes III. and Sety I. to lift the blocks to their
appointed places ; and Karnak has now been put, so far
as such a building can ever be put, into a condition of
reasonable security by the same methods which helped
its erection in the beginning.

So huge a building, of course, requires constant
attention ; and it was in the course of his labours in this
work of preservation that Legrain discovered on the
south side of the Hypostyle Hall what has come to be
known as " the Karnak *Cachette*," one of the most
wonderful collections of Egyptian sculpture which has
ever rewarded investigation. The find was made
during the extraction from the ground of one of the
limestone blocks of the long-ruined XIIth Dynasty
chapel of the Theban Ptah. When the block was lifted,
fragments of an alabaster colossus appeared, and when
these were removed, the workmen found more and
more pieces of sculpture beneath their feet in the mud
caused by the infiltration of Nile water. Before the
great pit had been emptied, literally hundreds of statues
and fragments of statues dating from the XVIIIth and
XIXth Dynasties and down to the Persian conquest
had been drawn from its muddy depths. In such a
mass of material, of course, there was a good deal of
comparatively poor work, interesting only from the
archæological point of view ; but a number of the
pieces were of first-rate importance, both artistically

1. HEAD OF SETY I.
2. GOLDFACED INNER MUMMY CASE OF QUEEN NEFERTARI.
3. HEAD OF RAMSES II.

PROFILE OF RAMSES II.
HEAD OF PIRETEM II.

and historically. Among the most precious specimens were a fine relief of Senusert I. of the XIIth Dynasty with the god Ptah, and a colossal pink granite head of Senusert III., showing the same strong harsh features as are seen in the grey granite statues found at Der el-Bahri, an extraordinarily fine portrait in green schist of Thothmes III., showing a strong and bold profile which accords infinitely better with one's idea of the great conqueror than the coarse brutality of the great colossal head in the British Museum, a fine portrait of the ancient sage Amenhotep the son of Hapi, and a figure made entirely of green felspar.

The question of how this great dump of discarded Pharaohs, priests, and nobles came into existence is one of interest. The reason appears to be something like this. We know that the Ptolemies did a great amount of building and re-building at Karnak, and we also know that these statues were buried during the Ptolemaic Period, for coins of that period were found in the pit. In the course of their work they must have inevitably found that the courts which they were restoring were encumbered with countless " ex-voto " statues, many of them more or less defaced and injured, many of them of men who were almost forgotten. It was impossible to smash them up, or to use them as building material, for they had been dedicated in the temple of Amen, and were therefore sacred. The problem was solved by digging this great pit within the sacred precincts, and consigning to its depths all the statues that the Ptolemies had no use for above-ground. We may be very thankful for the expedient, for the statue-dump has kept its treasures for us in far better condition than they would ·probably have presented had they been left standing in the courts of the temple, exposed to all the ravages of time, war, and tourists.

We have already seen, in de Morgan's find of the jewellery of the XIIth Dynasty princesses at Dahshur, the evidence of the skill of the Egyptian jewellers and goldsmiths of the Middle Kingdom. Further evidence in this direction came to light in February, 1914, during Petrie's work at Lahun, near the ruined pyramid of Senusert II. The workmen were clearing the already rifled tomb of " the Royal daughter Sat-Hathor-ant," when they came upon a store of fine gold and jewel work, not inferior in quality to the diadems of Khnumit in the earlier find. How this treasure had escaped the early tomb-robbers was a marvel and a mystery. " The whole treasure," says Petrie, " was standing in an open recess, within arm's reach of the gold-seekers, while they·worked at breaking open the granite sarcophagus." Our knowledge of the history and art of Egypt has so many gaps in it due to the greed and violence of the robber that we may be thankful that for once in a way he was thwarted, and left these priceless relics to be discovered by an age which can appreciate them at their true value.

The most remarkable piece of the Lahun treasure was a perfect example of a royal crown, with the uræus adorning its front. The Lahun crown is not the curious " Double-Crown " of Egypt, familiar to us from countless representations ; but what may be regarded as a kind of queen's diadem, infinitely less cumbrous and more beautiful than the more famous emblem. It is simply a broad band of highly burnished gold, over an inch wide, ornamented with fifteen golden rosettes of floral pattern. The uræus in front is of open-work and inlaid with lazuli and carnelian. From the back of the circlet rose a plume formed of two feathers of thin sheet gold, which would wave slightly with every motion of the head, and from the back and sides streamers of gold hung down from hinges attached to the rosettes.

Along with the crown were found two pectorals of even finer design and execution than those discovered at Dahshur, several jewelled collars and necklets, and broad armlets of gold and inlaid stones, bearing the royal cartouche, together with a number of amulets and toilet utensils, including a fine silver mirror with an obsidian handle, which was inlaid with bands of twisted gold, and bore a cast golden head of Hathor. In 1920 the complement to this great find came to light at Lahun, in the shape of the gold uræus of Senusert II., a heavy gold casting with a head of lazuli, and eyes of garnet set in gold, and inlay of carnelian and lazuli. The evidence of the Lahun Treasure underlined that of the Dahshur discovery as to the height reached by Egyptian civilisation in the Middle Kingdom. Such triumphs of design and workmanship spoke to a refinement of taste worthy of the best periods of a great nation's history, while the richness of the whole equipment bore testimony to the command of ample resources ; and altogether the effect of the find was to confirm the growing impression that the time of the XIth and XIIth Dynasties must be regarded as one of the great culminating periods of Egyptian development. The period of the early dynasties, from Mena to the close of the VIth Dynasty, the time of the Middle Kingdom, and that of the New Empire under the XVIIIth Dynasty—these may be regarded as the successive points when the tide of Egyptian prosperity and culture was at its flood.

M

In 1914 the Davis concession in the Valley of the Kings was abandoned, and the right to continue the excavations in the Valley was granted to the Earl of Carnarvon and Mr. Howard Carter, who had been working in the Theban Necropolis since 1907, with comparatively little success. Nor was there any great expectation on the part of the officials of the Service of Antiquities that this new effort would be rewarded with any conspicuous result ; for the general opinion was that the Valley had now yielded up all, or almost all, its treasures. The new workers, however, thought otherwise, for various reasons, among others the fact that a number of small finds had been made at different times of articles bearing the cartouche of Tutankhamen, one of the sons-in-law and successors of Akhenaten, the heretic Pharaoh of Tell el-Amarna. It was not till the autumn of 1917 that the real attempt to work the concession began ; and for six campaigns the excavations were carried on with a depressing lack of success. In fact the excavators were almost on the point of abandoning their task in despair. There remained, however, one small area, beneath the tomb of Ramses VI., which had not yet been attacked, partly because of the fact that operations in this area might interfere with the access of tourists to the tomb of the XXth Dynasty king, which is one of the show tombs of the Valley. It was now resolved to make a last attempt in this area, and the work had not been well begun before success beyond the utmost hopes of the excavators rewarded their patience.

Excavation began under Mr. Howard Carter's direction on November 1st, 1922 ; and on the morning of November 4th, Mr. Carter, on arriving at the scene of

A LIFE-SIZE WOODEN IMAGE OF TUTANKHAMEN FOUND IN THE FIRST
CHAMBER OF HIS TOMB.

(The Times world copyright, by arrangement with the Earl of Carnarvon.)

work, was greeted with the information that a rock-cut step had been uncovered. Further excavation revealed the fact that this was the beginning of a steep stairway. By November 6th, the top of a doorway, blocked with stones, plastered and sealed, began to appear ; and at last the whole stairway of sixteen steps, with the sealed door at the foot of it, was cleared, and there could no longer be any doubt that an important discovery lay under the explorer's hands. At this stage work was stopped for a time to allow of the arrival of Lord Carnarvon ; but on the 25th the work was resumed, the first sealed door broken through, and a sloping passage revealed, at the foot of which, when it had been cleared of the rubble with which it was filled, there appeared another sealed doorway. Next day brought the answer to the question whether triumph or another disappointment lay ahead.

"The decisive moment had arrived," says Mr. Carter. "With trembling hands I made a tiny breach in the upper left-hand corner. . . . At first I could see nothing, the hot air escaping from the chamber causing the candle to flicker, but presently, as my eyes grew accustomed to the light, details of the room within emerged slowly from the mist, strange animals, statues, and gold—everywhere the glint of gold. For the moment—an eternity it must have seemed to the others standing by—I was struck dumb with amazement, and when Lord Carnarvon, unable to stand the suspense any longer, inquired anxiously, ' Can you see anything ? ' it was all I could do to get out the words, ' Yes, wonderful things.' Then widening the hole a little further, so that we both could see, we inserted an electric torch."

Mr. Carter's agitation was only natural. Never, not even in the great find of Pharaohs at Der el-Bahri,

forty-one years before, had such wealth of precious
material met the eye of any explorer.   In the comparatively small chamber through which the explorers
cautiously picked their way, there was no appearance
of any burial, royal or otherwise ; but even the treasures
of the tomb of Yuaa and Tuau seemed insignificant in
comparison with the piles of coffers, state couches,
gilded chairs, footstools, alabaster vases, shrines, chariots,
and other objects which met the bewildered eyes of the
men who had accomplished this strange resurrection of
the past.   At one end of the chamber stood, facing one
another, two life-sized statues of Tutankhamen, the
Pharaoh to whom all this splendour had belonged, carved
in bituminised wood, and adorned with gold.   They
seemed to be watching over the partition-wall, plastered
and sealed, which closed this side of the room, and
gave promise of something else beyond it.   Conspicuous
among the heaps of treasure were three great gilt couches,
their sides carved into the shape of monstrous creatures,
whose hideous heads arose above the ends of the frames.
At the foot of one of the statues lay a coffer painted with
the most exquisite art with scenes of the King's warfare
and hunting—a piece of artistic work which would in
itself have been an ample reward for the labour which
had brought it to light.   Under one of the couches
stood a magnificent state chair, the ends of its arms
carved into the shape of lions' heads, while the whole
fabric of it was plated with gold.   The back of this
marvel of craftsmanship was adorned with a panel on
which the king and his wife Ankh. s. en. Amen are
represented in polychrome faience, and glass and stone
inlay.   Other discoveries had made us familiar with the
skill of the Egyptian craftsman of the XVIIIth Dynasty

in the designing and execution of beautiful furniture ;
but no such wonderful example of what he was capable
of had ever before been seen.   Other chairs, only less
beautiful and gorgeous, lay around, while in one corner
of the room there was a pile of chariots, dismantled in
order to enable them to pass through the doorway of
the tomb, but complete in all their details. Boxes,
coffers, and caskets of all shapes, and all kinds of material,
but all of exquisite shape and workmanship, were stuffed
with linen, and all kinds of things for royal use, among
them the king's sandals, of gold filigree work and inlay,
and his bows and walking-sticks, wonderfully carved,
and inlaid.

Beneath one of the couches, a small hole in the
partition wall gave access to another chamber, a kind
of annexe to the first, which it was impossible even to
enter, for it was literally packed to a height of several
feet with other treasures. At the bottom of the end
wall, between the two statues, a piece of wall which had
been re-plastered and re-sealed showed that in ancient
days the tomb had been violated and robbed, to what
extent only further investigation could prove.

After the first feeling of bewilderment had somewhat
passed, there came the question of what plan should
be followed in dealing with all the mass of priceless
material already revealed, and what course of action
should be adopted with reference to the prosecution of
further investigation. It was manifest that behind the
sealed wall there must lie another chamber, probably
the actual tomb-chamber of the king. Was it to be
opened also, and the whole extent of the discovery un-
veiled at once ? The temptation must have been strong
upon the explorers to make sure of what they had actually

found, and the lure of the sealed wall must have been hard to resist. But the claims of the mass of wonderful material which lay actually under their hands were paramount. To carry on further operations involving the breaking down of the partition wall before the treasures in hand were secured and placed in safety meant almost inevitably that some of the articles in the chamber would be destroyed, and others damaged. It was resolved, therefore, to postpone the breaking of the sealed wall until the antechamber had been sufficiently cleared to ensure that no damage would be done to its contents by the operations.

Accordingly the empty tomb of Sety II. was converted into a store-house and laboratory where the contents of the antechamber could be housed and treated with preservatives, and the tomb of Queen Tiy, in which the coffin and bones of Akhenaten were found by Mr. Davis, was brought into service as a photographic dark-room, and for several weeks the work of clearing the chamber proceeded under the eyes of an endless throng of tourists, until at last it was judged that it was safe to venture on the further search, and to prove if the faith of the explorers would be justified that beyond the wall there lay the practically intact funerary equipment of a Pharaoh of the New Empire, with his mummy in the midst of it.

The day appointed for the actual breaking through of the wall was Friday, February 16th, 1923, though the formal ceremony of opening the inner chamber did not take place till two days later. A company of about twenty privileged persons, among them several famous experts, was invited to witness the work. Ten minutes' work opened a hole large enough to enable Mr. Carter

THE PAINTED CASKET SHOWING TUTANKHAMEN IN THE FORM OF ANDRO-
SPHINXES TRAMPLING UPON HIS AFRICAN ENEMIES. THE ANDRO-
SPHINX HAS A HUMAN HEAD UPON A LION'S BODY, TYPIFYING THE
UNION OF INTELLECTUAL AND PHYSICAL POWER.

THE SECRET OF THE INNER CHAMBER REVEALED, SHOWING A LARGE
PORTION OF THE SHRINE.

THE TOMB OF TUTANKHAMEN.

to peer through ; and when he did so he was faced with what seemed to be a solid wall of gold stretching from one end of the inner chamber to the other. The hole was quickly enlarged, and as stone after stone was removed it became evident that this golden wall was part of a gigantic shrine, covered with gold and faience inlay, and adorned with sacred emblems, chiefly the Pillar of Osiris and the Buckle of Isis. It was well known, both from the evidence of the illustrations in various papyri, and from the portions of the actual shrines which had come to light in different excavations, notably the fragments of those of Queen Astenkheb, and Queen Tiy, that each Pharaoh was laid to rest in his stone sarcophagus under several such canopies ; but never before had a complete specimen of the funeral canopy of a Pharaoh greeted the eyes of any excavator. The sight was such as fairly to make all the spectators gasp with amazement. The canopy was seventeen feet long, by eleven broad, and nine high, and almost completely filled the room in which it stood, leaving only a narrow passage between it and the rock-walls, which were adorned with somewhat indifferent decorative work. At the north end of the shrine lay the seven oars which the royal voyager would require for his journey across the waters of the Underworld. At the eastern end were two great doors, closed and bolted, but not sealed. These were opened, and within appeared a second canopy, covered entirely with gold, and closed with doors whose bolts were secured by intact seals. Between the two shrines a great pall of linen covered with golden rosettes dropped above the inner one. The doors of the outer canopy were closed again and bolted, and the explorers resumed their investigation of the tomb-chamber.

At its further end they found that a low doorway, which had never been closed, gave access to yet another room ; and here manifestly lay some of the greatest treasures of the whole marvellous find. Opposite the doorway stood a shrine which Mr. Carter has described as " the most beautiful monument that I have ever seen— so lovely that it made one gasp with wonder and admiration." It was a large coffer shaped like a shrine, overlaid with gold, and provided with the regular cornice of sacred cobras. Surrounding this shrine, and not carved in relief on it, as in other cases, but standing free, were four guardian goddesses with outstretched arms. Those in front and behind the shrine had their eyes fixed upon their charge ; but the other two had their heads turned sideways towards the door, as if watching against any surprise, and reproaching the intruder. In all probability this is the Canopic chest, which contains the four jars with the vital organs of the dead king ; and from the artistic point of view it is one of the supreme triumphs of the Egyptian artist.

Immediately in front of the entrance lay the customary figure of the couchant Jackal-god Anubis, the Guide of the Dead through the ways of the Underworld, and the whole room was filled with shrines and coffers of all shapes and sizes, some of them containing, no doubt, the funerary statuettes of the king. In different parts of the room lay several model-boats completely rigged, and yet another chariot ; while in one casket whose lid the explorers raised, there lay a beautiful ostrich-feather fan with ivory handle, in perfect condition.

Such were the impressions made on the minds of the first intruders on the long rest of Tutankhamen by their brief glimpse of the dead monarch's glories. They were followed into the inner chamber by the rest of the party, who had been anxiously waiting. " It was curious," says Mr. Carter, " as we stood in the ante-chamber, to watch their faces, as, one by one, they emerged from the door. Each had a dazed, bewildered look in his eyes, and each in turn as he came out, threw up his hands before him, an unconscious gesture of impotence to describe in words the wonders that he had seen." A week later the tomb was again closed beneath hundreds of tons of rubbish, and Tutankhamen was left to sleep in peace for a few months longer. Ere long a new touch of pathos was added to the story of the great discovery by the illness and death of Lord Carnarvon, who died in Cairo on April 6th, 1923.

The work of re-opening the tomb and completing the examination of its treasures was resumed by Mr. Carter in November, 1923. His first task was the dismantling of the great outer canopy which obviously had been brought in sections into the tomb and there assembled over the other shrines and the sarcophagus. This task proved to be an unexpectedly difficult one, owing to the weight of the different sections, and the thorough manner in which they had been jointed together by the Egyptian joiners of 3,300 years ago. After a considerable portion of the shrine had been removed, it was possible to roll the linen pall with its gold rosettes away from the second canopy ; and this delicate operation was carried out with extreme care, for the pall was in a very fragile condition, and the weight of the rosettes threatened to prove too much for the integrity of the fabric. At last the pall was cleared away and the framework on which it had rested removed ; and it now became possible to open the sealed doors of the second shrine, and to see what lay within. On January 3rd, 1924, the ebony bolts were carefully drawn through the bronze staples, after the sealed cord which secured them had been cut. The doors were then opened, and a third golden shrine was disclosed, its doors also fastened with ebony bolts, secured with cord and seal, the seal in this instance bearing the cartouche of Tutankhamen as well as the familiar jackal and nine captives of the Royal Necropolis. Again the seal-cord was cut and the bolts drawn ; and when the doors of this third canopy were swung open, it was to reveal a fourth, whose doors were adorned with figures of the guardian goddesses. The bolts of this fourth shrine were shot, but not sealed ; and when they were drawn and the doors opened, they disclosed a great sarcophagus of red crystalline sandstone, evidently intact, and with its heavy lid still securely in place. The corners of the great coffin were guarded, as in the case of the pink granite sarcophagus of Horemheb, with the figures of four goddesses in relief, stretching out their wings in protection along the sides of the coffin.

The knowledge for which the shrines had been opened at this point had now been obtained. It was known that the sarcophagus lay within, and was intact, and some idea could also now be formed of the size of the block of stone which formed the lid, and of what measures would have to be adopted to raise it in the cramped space of the tomb-chamber. Therefore the investigation of the contents of the shrines went no further at this stage, and the explorers returned to the difficult and monotonous task of dismantling the remainder of the outer shrine. There the matter rests at the moment of writing, and it will probably be a

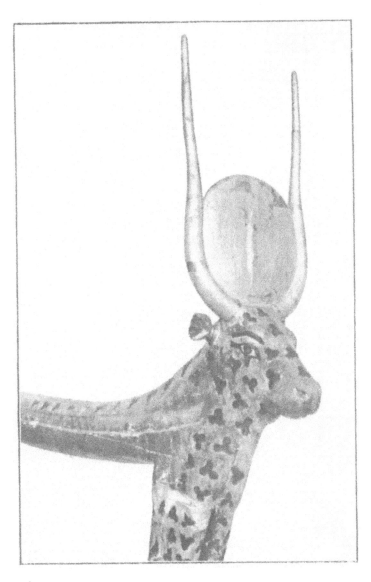

THE HEAD OF THE HATHOR COUCH.

(The Times world copyright photograph by Mr. Harry Burton.)

considerable time before the work advances to the stage when the lid of the sarcophagus can be lifted and its contents revealed. What revelations await us, we may imagine, but cannot say with certainty. There can be little doubt that it is an untouched royal interment which lies beneath the shrines ; as to anything more we can only conjecture in the meantime. Reasoning on the ground afforded to us by previous experience, it would seem likely that the stone sarcophagus will be found to hold within it at least two wooden coffins, carved, painted, and gilded, probably with a modelled head of the dead king upon each. Within the innermost of these will be the mummy, very possibly not only swathed in its wrappings, but also covered from head to foot with a perfect armour of amulets in gold, and precious and semi-precious stones. It has been suggested that the full regalia of Egypt may be buried with the king, and that now we may have the chance of actually seeing the quaint " Double Crown," the curious and cumbrous sort of composite mitre which the Egyptian monarch wore to symbolise his lordship over " The Two Lands "—Upper and Lower Egypt, along with the different sceptres, and other articles of royal dignity which were part of the equipment of a Pharaoh on great occasions of state. That, however, is matter of conjecture only. With a reasonable amount of certainty we may expect that several papyri may be found on the breast or upon the thighs of the dead king, and that these will be of the highest value as fine specimens of the art of writing and illumination ; but the chances are against their containing anything of historical importance, or anything that will add to our scanty knowledge of the reign of Tutankhamen. Funerary papyri are invariably limited in their scope to the function for which they were placed beside the dead man, and contain nothing but the chapters of the Book of the Dead, or other kindred works which were supposed to be useful to the departed on his journey through the Underworld.   There may be the chance, indeed, of finding some such roll of magic as that book of Thoth for which Na-nefer-ka-ptah paid so dear, and which Setna-Khaemuast tried in vain to keep from its rightful owner ; but on the whole the likelihood is that whatever papyri are found will be of a purely ritual character, and valuable more from the point of their execution than for any addition which they may make to our knowledge of either Egyptian history or literature.

Such, in brief outline, are some of the main features of Egyptian research work during the forty-two years which have elapsed since the new period opened with the reign of Maspero at the Service of Antiquities and the find of the Der el-Bahri *cache*. To have attempted to cover the whole ground would simply have resulted in this chapter becoming a string of names of explorers, and the sites of their excavations, and accordingly only the most outstanding, and perhaps in some instances the most picturesque, have been selected for discussion ; but enough has been said to show that even in these days, when Crete and Greece, Mesopotamia and Anatolia are all revealing to us treasures of the ancient world of the highest interest and importance, Egypt still holds her own, and has the power not only to present us with results inferior in importance to none of those which other lands are yielding, but also to touch all that she yields with a romance of which the old Empire of the Nile alone can claim the secret.

J. B.

CHAPTER V

EGYPT TO SINAI

THE traveller in Egypt or Palestine finds himself everywhere surrounded by the traces of a long and diversified series of events of the utmost interest and importance. Commencing with the very dawn of history, they continued to run their course, not merely for centuries, but for millenniums, and have been recorded on imperishable monuments, or in yet more imperishable writings. The ever-varying aspects of nature in those countries serve to illustrate and explain the great drama of their history. We can see how the course of human affairs was modified or determined by the conditions of physical geography. The sea, the rivers, the mountains, the desert, all had their influence upon the development of the Hebrew and the Egyptian people, and were employed for the accomplishment of His purposes, by Him who " hath made of one blood all nations of men for to dwell on all the face of the earth, and hath determined the times before appointed, and the bounds of their habitation." [1]

Lying between these two countries—between them, not only geographically but historically—is a district

[1] Acts xvii. 26.

which is in striking contrast to both. The Sinaitic peninsula was the route by which the Israelites passed from Egypt into Palestine, and it formed the birthplace and cradle of the nation. They entered it a horde of fugitive slaves. They left it fused and welded into an organic whole, which continues down to our own day. And it is this solitary fact which gives to it its sole claim on our attention. A solemn and impressive monotony is the characteristic of the region. History records but a single event. Nature offers but a single aspect unchanged from age to age. At certain seasons of the year " a thin and transparent veil of greyish green " is drawn over portions of the soil. Here and there a clump of palms, tamarisks, and acacias may be found. A few wells of bitter, brackish water attract the wandering Bedouin with their flocks and herds. We shall hereafter see reasons for believing that at the period of the Exodus the population of the peninsula was more numerous, and its soil somewhat more fertile, than now. But with these exceptions it is " a waste howling wilderness " of bare rocks, intersected by *wâdies* of sterile sand, gravel, and marl, without history and without change.

In attempting to trace the route of the children of Israel from Egypt to Sinai, we are beset by difficulties which almost preclude the possibility of a definite or satisfactory conclusion.

We have already seen that the boundary-line between Egypt and the desert is uncertain and fluctuating, dependent not on fixed and natural, but on varying and artificial, conditions. It is determined by the energy with which irrigation is carried out. The conflict between the fertilising river and the encroaching sand—between Osiris and Typhon, as the old mythology symbolised it

—is conducted with ever-varying alternations of victory and defeat. Under the Pharaohs and the Ptolemies, canals had pushed the frontier of Egypt forward into districts which are now utterly desolate and barren. Recent discoveries enable us to fix, with tolerable certainty, the site of Raamses, which formed the starting-point of the Exodus. But at the present day Raamses lies outside the limits of cultivation, and is buried beneath the sands of the desert. Where was Succoth—*the shepherds' booths*—which formed the first halting-place ? And where was " Etham, which is in the edge of the wilderness " ? [1] In the changed condition of the country we can discover no premisses to warrant a positive conclusion as to these important sites. The question is still further complicated by geological changes in the isthmus. The Red Sea formerly extended much farther to the north than at present. An upheaval of the soil has cut off the district now known as the Bitter Lakes from the head of the Gulf of Suez. And there is some evidence to prove that this upheaval has taken place at a period subsequent to the Exodus. It is then possible, perhaps even probable, that Pi-hahiroth, Migdol, and Baal-zephon must be sought for, not where the present coast-line of the Red Sea would indicate, but many miles to the north of where the town of Suez now stands. After a careful balancing of the arguments adduced by Eyptologists and Biblical expositors, I come to the conclusion that this is the case. Without presuming to dogmatise upon so difficult and complicated a problem, the theory which places the line of transit through the sea somewhere near Shaloof, a station on the canal about fifteen miles north of Suez, seems to me to have the greatest weight

[1] Exodus xii. 37 ; xiii. 20. Numbers xxxiii. 5–7.

of evidence in its favour.[1] We thus adopt the cogent arguments of Brugsch and others as to the line of route, and escape the difficulty of supposing, with them, that the passage was through the Serbonian Bog, or the Bitter Lakes, instead of through the sea, as the narrative evidently requires.

A yet further difficulty in the way of tracing the course pursued by the fugitives arises from the character of the only historical document we possess on the subject. The Mosaic narrative is one of remarkable precision and accuracy. It is, in fact, an itinerary giving the journeys day by day, and the halting-places night by night.[2] But, as Dean Stanley has remarked, it was written by and for those who were so well acquainted with the localities that they required no explanatory details. The names being familiar and the places known, no further indication was thought needful. This, whilst it affords a strong incidental corroboration of the authenticity of the narrative, deprives us of those helps to identify the stations on the route which might otherwise have been afforded. The names having disappeared, or being only

[1] Professor Hull, the head of the geological expedition sent out to this region by the Palestine Exploration Fund in 1883, confirms this view. He says (*Mount Seir*, page 37): "The waters of the Red and, I may add, the Mediterranean Sea, extended over the lands of Egypt and along the shore of the Gulf of Suez to a height of over two hundred feet above the present level of these waters, at a time when the existing species of shells were already living. The process of elevation of this sea-bed over so large a tract was probably exceedingly gradual, and at the date of the Exodus the elevation may not have taken place up to the present extent. A strip of Red Sea water—not very deep—may at this time have stretched from the Gulf of Suez as far north as the Great Bitter Lake, forming to the host of Israel an effective barrier to their progress into the desert. The passage may have taken place to the north of the present head of the Gulf of Suez."

See also the chapter, "The Geography of the Exodus," in Sir William Dawson's *Egypt and Syria*, By-Paths of Bible Knowledge, No. VI.   [2] Numbers xxxiii. 5–37.

handed down by doubtful and obscure traditions, we are left to work out a conjectural line of march from insufficient data.

But whatever perplexities we may feel in the endeavour to trace the precise course followed by the Israelites, the general outlines of the scenery remain unchanged, and we can realise with the utmost vividness and certainty the general aspect of the country through which they passed. The Sinaitic peninsula is divided into two main portions. The northern, known as the Badiet et Tih, or Desert of the Wandering, is a vast triangular plateau of limestone, which runs down to a point in the centre of the peninsula. It has no marked features and no historical associations. Notwithstanding its name, we have no evidence that the Israelites actually crossed it, though in the course of their forty years' wanderings they may have done so. On their journey southward from Egypt to Sinai, they kept along its western edge between the Jebel et Tih and the Gulf of Suez and on their northward journey from Sinai to Canaan they skirted its south-eastern corner. Separated from this northern plateau by a belt of sand, the Debet er Ramleh, and stretching away in the south, is a chaos of mountain peaks—sandstone and granite—some of which rise to a height of nearly 9,000 feet. In winter the higher summits are capped with snow. With this exception, they are for the most part absolutely bare. The splintered savage tors, denuded of soil, have been compared to a sea running mountains high and suddenly petrified into solid immovable masses. Tempests of frightful violence often rage among them. Lightning leaps from crag to crag. Peals of thunder seem to shake the earth. Torrents of rain descend, and, forming cascades, sweep

N

all before them with destructive fury. The *wâdies*, or valleys, which intersect these mountain ranges are covered with marl or gravel, generally strewn with granite boulders. Clumps of broom, acacia, willow, tamarisk and wild palm, with here and there a cypress, are found springing from the arid soil. Sage and other aromatic shrubs afford a meagre pasture for the camels, flocks, and herds of the Bedouin. Wells or pools of brackish water are not infrequent. And there are a few oases where the date-palm grows luxuriantly along the banks of some running stream which wells forth from a cleft in the rocks, but is soon absorbed by the thirsty earth. This sparse and meagre vegetation, however, is not sufficient to dissipate the general aspect of barrenness and desolation which the wilderness presents.

Following in the track of the Israelites, we leave Suez, and in about three hours reach the Ayûn Mûsa, or Wells of Moses. These wells are of all shapes and sizes. Some are merely shallow pools, others are deep shafts lined with masonry. In most of them the water is bitter and acrid ; in a few only is it drinkable. Aquatic plants cover the surface of the ponds, and the surrounding soil is laid out in gardens which are irrigated by sâkiyehs like those used in Egypt. If we adopt the theory that the passage of the Israelites through the Red Sea was at a point to the north of the present head of the Gulf, Ayûn Mûsa may with some probability be identified as Marah, " where they could not drink of the waters, for they were bitter." [1]

The route southward from Ayûn Mûsa leads along the shore over gravelly plains many miles broad, which slope upward from the sea to the mountains of the Tih.

[1] Exodus xv. 23.

After heavy rains the stiff tenacious marl is pitted with numerous pools of water, and is sprinkled with the aromatic shrubs which constitute the flora of the desert. But the scorching sun soon dries up the pools, and the

WELLS OF MOSES.

short-lived plants wither into dust. Several wells of bitter water are passed, each of which has been fixed upon as Marah, according to the view taken of the place of passage. About fifty miles south of Ayûn Mûsa the Wâdy Gharandel is reached.[1] The entrance into the

[1] It was in a valley running down from the Tih, not far from Ayûn Mûsa, that Professor Palmer and Lieutenant Gill were

valley, or wâdy, is not much over eighty feet wide, and on either side grey-looking cliffs of gritstone rise with ragged faces to a considerable height. But that which adds so great a charm to the scene is an actual stream of water, rippling along, silvery and bright, garnished on each bank with luxuriant plants that thrive and flourish in the wet sand. Forget-me-nots peep out from amidst the sedgy grass reeds and mint that tower above the water ; while some kind of brook plant, like a tangled mat, spreads itself over the sandy edges of the rivulet and sends its long arms, tufted with rootlets at every joint, out into the running water. Here the vegetation takes quite a different character. The spiny acacia, the *sumt* of the Arabs, probably the tree of the " burning bush " and the shittim wood of the tabernacle, grows plentifully ; but, spiny though it be, it has to bear its burden of climbing plants, being generally quite hidden beneath their twisting, rope-like branches. Conspicuous amongst the larger plants is the *retem*, or wild broom, handsome alike in growth and foliage. It is probably the shrub beneath which Elijah slept in his wanderings.

Date-palms of strangely stunted stature are scattered along the sandy banks ; one might readily mistake them for giant yuccas at a hasty glance, so much do they resemble those plants in their mode of growth. These may truly be called " *wild palms :* " dwarfed, and un- altered by man's hand. Was this the memorable place where " there were twelve wells of water and threescore and ten palm trees "—the veritable Elim of the Exodus ? Many travellers believe this wâdy to be the place.[1]

---

murdered by the Arabs in 1882. Many are of opinion that the deed was due to orders issued by Arabi Pasha.

[1] Exodus xv. 27.

SINAITIC INSCRIPTIONS.

Striking eastward up the wâdy we soon reach the traces of mines worked by the ancient Egyptians. Hieroglyphic tablets are found in considerable numbers, one of which contains the name of Cheops, the builder of the Great Pyramid, and some are said to be even earlier.[1] At Serabit el Khadem, which seems to have been the capital of the mining district, are some remarkable ruins, consisting of a temple, the remains of houses, and perhaps a necropolis. Fragments of columns, blocks of stone, pieces of rude sculpture, and mounds of broken pottery lie scattered about in perplexing confusion. The upright blocks, or stelæ, are amongst the most curious parts of the present ruin. They are from eight to ten feet in height, rounded at the top, and fairly well faced. The rock from which they are hewn is a compact sandstone, and they do not appear to be distributed with any regard to uniformity of distances or position. Thickly covering both sides are hieroglyphic inscriptions. This is but one of the many traces of ancient settlements to be found in this part of the peninsula, which seem clearly to prove that it must have been more thickly populated, and therefore more fertile, in former ages than at present. It is important to bear this fact in mind, as it confutes one of the main arguments brought by infidels against the truth of the Mosaic narrative. Where, it has been asked, could pasture have been found for the " flocks and herds, and very much cattle " brought up by the Israelites out of Egypt, and which served for sacrifices in the wilderness ? [2] Whence came the Amalekites and other nations who fought against Israel, and threatened to

---

[1] The earliest tablet is that of Semerkhet of the Ist Dynasty in the Wâdy Maghara. It antedates Khufu by at least 500 years.

[2] Exodus xii. 38 ; xxiv. 5.

destroy them ? [1] These sceptical questions, like others of a similar class, are based upon an entire misapprehension of the facts. We only need more accurate knowledge to discover a triumphant answer. That the general aspect of the desert must always have been what we now see is indeed certain. But no less certain is it that the oases which still exist were once far more numerous, fertile, and densely populated than now.[2]

In the same district is the Wâdy Mokatteb, or the Written Valley, so called from the number of rude inscriptions and sculptures with which the rocks are covered. They are not peculiar to this valley, but are found in many other parts of the Sinaitic range. They always occur in the lines of route along which caravans of traders or bands of pilgrims are likely to have passed, and are inscribed in the soft sandstone rock which forms the fringe of the harder granite in the centre of the peninsula. The sculptures are grotesque representations of birds, camels, asses, horses, ibexes, and other animals. The inscriptions are sometimes in Greek, Latin, or Hebrew, but more commonly in a character unlike that of any known language. Up to a recent date, the several opinions held regarding the origin of these writings resolve themselves into two : the one that they were the work of the Israelites during their sojourn in the

---

[1] Exodus xvii. 8–15.

[2] Professor Petrie's conclusion is as follows : " There does not seem, then, to be any evidence of a perceptible change of climate in Sinai, any more than in Egypt ; if there be a change, it is rather that of increase than of decrease in the rainfall. If, then, the climate is unaltered, the maximum population must be unaltered." *Researches in Sinai*, p. 207. The temple and steles at Serabit el-Khadem are the relics left by the various expeditions of the Ancient Egyptians, who visited the district at intervals for the purpose of mining copper and turquoise. There was never any settled occupation of the place.

desert ; the other that they were the pastime of Christian shepherds who were permanent residents, or possibly of Christian pilgrims in search of Mount Sinai. This *quæstio vexata* was settled by the discoveries of the late Professor Palmer, who showed that the character is simply " another phase of that Semitic alphabet whose forms appear alike in the Hebrew, Arabic and Greek," or, as it may be explained in other words, constitutes an intermediate link betwixt the Cufic and ordinary Hebrew. Professor Beer refers to a stone in Wâdy Mokatteb on which there was a *bilingual* inscription ; Mr. Palmer also discovered it, and states that there can be no doubt that the Greek and Sinaitic writing of which the inscription consists was executed by the same hand. Nor is this a solitary instance. These writings, hitherto supposed to be of so great an age, are only detached sentences, in an Aramæan dialect, " a great many of them being proper names, with here and there introductory formulæ such as Oriental peoples have been from time immemorial accustomed to prefix to their compositions." They were probably the work of pilgrims and traders during the earlier part of the Christian era, or for two or three centuries before it. The Christian signs employed denote that many of the inscribers, were Christians ; but there is evidence to prove that a large proportion of them were Jews or Pagans. " The writing must have extended into the monkish times, possibly until the spread of El-Islám brought the ancestors of the present inhabitants, Bedouin hordes, from El-Hajaz and other parts of Arabia Proper, to the mountains of Sinai, and dispersed or absorbed that Saracen population of whom the monks stood in such mortal dread."

Leaving the Wâdy Mokatteb by a boulder-strewn

valley, we enter the Wâdy Feiran, the most beautiful and fertile of all the wâdies in the peninsula—perhaps the only one to which these epithets can properly be applied. Some years ago it was devastated by a frightful inundation caused by storms of unusual violence in the mountains, which turned the wâdy into a torrent ten feet in depth. Thirty Bedouin were drowned, hundreds of sheep and goats perished, and upwards of a thousand palm trees were uprooted and washed away. Many years must pass before the traces of this destructive deluge have disappeared.

At the entrance of the wâdy are the remains of some of those ancient buildings to which reference has already been made. Stone circles, and kist-vaens, curiously like those of our own early Celtic period, have been discovered. In some of the latter, opened by Mr. Lord, the bodies were found with the knees bent upon the chest, as was the case in all the tombs of this class examined by him throughout the peninsula. The significance of this fact will be understood by the students of pre-historic antiquities. In and around many of the graves flint implements have been found in considerable numbers, but none were seen in the Wâdy Feiran. About seven miles beyond these ruins the wâdy expands, while the rocks are lower, with wider watercourses intersecting their escarpments. Scrubby little date-palms begin to appear on the patches of alluvium, as if placed there to mark the frontier between sterility and verdure. Farther on, acacias and tamarisks, with palms of more stately mien, can be descried, resembling in the distance a coppice on a sandy plain. Several species of birds flit from bush to bush, some of them warbling as sweetly as an English song thrush ; the drowsy hum of insects falls pleasantly on the ear, while the eye experiences a delicious relief in resting upon the deep green foliage of the leafy trees.

A Bedouin settlement is now reached, occupied throughout the year by a number of slaves employed in cultivating the soil, and gathering and preparing the fruit of the date-palms. Many of them are negroes, others are of a lighter complexion, with thinner lips and less prominent cheekbones. Their Bedouin masters visit the spot at intervals to feast upon the products of this delightful oasis, which consist not only of dates, but grain, cucumbers, gourds, pomegranates, and lotuses, as well as large quantities of sugar-cane and tobacco.

A narrow rocky gorge having been passed, we enter a sandy plain sparsely covered with stunted tamarisk bushes. On the slopes of the hills are seen ruins of ancient dwellings, proving the existence of numerous inhabitants at some former period. Here a magnificent view is gained of the grandest of all the mountains of the peninsula, Jebel Serbal. Seen from this spot, it presents to the eye of the observer a confused mass of peaks of varying heights, but in reality these are reducible to five well-marked ones, the others being more or less simply accessories. The mountain is composed of granite, and the peaks shoot up precipitously from the basement like so many columns.

Turning a sharp angle of rock which juts out far enough into the wâdy to hide the upper palm-grove, a wonderful scene of enchantment suddenly bursts upon the view. On each side, and to all appearance completely shutting in this part of Wâdy Feiran from the world beyond it, immense cliffs of bare granite rock seem to tower up into the very clouds. Beneath the shadows of these frowning precipices a vast plantation of date-palms flourishes in the richest luxuriance. Through the centre of the grove a rivulet of sparkling water trickles along, anon eddying mysteriously beneath the gnarled roots of a patriarchal pine, as though coyly hiding, but soon dancing out again to the music of its own murmuring ripple. The " laughing water " rushes past the tangled clusters of wild mint, coquetting with the blue forget-me-nots, kissing the green fronds of the dangling sedge grass, then tumbling at last in a miniature cascade over a low ledge of rock, is sucked up and consumed by the thirsty sand of the desert. Along the banks of sand and alluvium through which the water has cut a wide channel, grow waving groups of tamarisk trees, while in the patches of cultivated ground the rich crimson blossoms of the pomegranate eclipse all beside in splendour of colour.

Feiran is clearly a modernised form of the ancient Paran—the surrounding wilderness being so called from this, the most important settlement in it—but as the name is applied in the Bible to the whole district stretching in a north-easterly direction to the borders of Canaan, it is difficult to fix upon any special site. The magnificent mass of Serbal which arises above the wâdy has been by some writers identified with Sinai—the Mountain of the Law—but upon insufficient grounds. With more probability the site of Rephidim has been sought in this valley. Here the Amalekites would be likely to make a stand for the defence of the most fertile spot in their territory. The fact that Serbal was a sacred mountain in very early times, and a place of pilgrimage and Pagan worship, gives point to the statement that Moses, with Aaron and Hur, " went up to the top of the hill," to pray, whilst the battle was raging in the valley, and explains the language of Jethro : " Now know I that Jehovah is greater than all gods." On the very spot where these idol deities were worshipped, the servants of the Lord call upon Him for help, and He proves His power by giving them the victory.[1] The only objection to this identification arises from the want of water.[2] The difficulty, however, is not insuperable. We may suppose, either that the host had only reached the lower part of the valley, which is barren and waterless, whilst the Amalekites barred the progress upward, or that, in a season of drought, the usual abundant supply had failed, as often happens in the present day.

"And they departed from Rephidim, and pitched in the wilderness of Sinai, . . . and there Israel encamped before the mount."[3] If Feiran is rightly identified as Rephidim, the route of the Israelites would be by the Wâdy esh Sheikh. This is a broad and noble valley shut in by mighty hills, and in many parts shadowed by groves of tamarisk trees. Its southern extremity opens into the Wâdy ed Deir, which runs to the south-west, and forms a right angle with the great plain Er Râhah. This is probably the wilderness of Sinai spoken of in the quotation just given from the Book of Exodus. The wâdy turns sharply to the right, and is contracted to a narrow gorge between the mountains. About half-way up this gorge is the monastery of St. Catherine, as it is commonly called, though really it is dedicated to the Transfiguration. Its ordinary name is due to the tradi-tional tomb of the saint which it contains.

The convent was founded by Justinian (A.D. 527),

---

[1] Exodus xvii. 8–15 ; xviii. 11.   [2] Exodus xvii. 1–6.
[3] Numbers xxxiii. 15. Exodus xix. 1, 2.

and was originally higher up the side of the mountain, perhaps even on the summit. It now lies at the base of Jebel Mûsa, in a narrow part of the valley surrounded by gardens, which are cultivated by the monks and their Arab servants. Until recently it resembled a beleaguered fortress rather than a convent. The only admission to it was gained by means of an aperture high up in the wall. Visitors were hoisted up by means of a crane, the windlass being worked by the monks inside. The most dignified personages had thus to submit to be treated like bales of goods. Recently the Bedouin, having become friendly with the monks, and the number of visitors having increased, a gateway has been opened, though the strong iron-clamped door is still jealously guarded.[1]

As the sale of manna forms an important item in the income of the monastery, this seems the proper place to inquire whether what now passes under that name is really the same with the manna of the Israelites. That it is the same, and that the miracle consisted in an enormous increase of the quantity produced, has been maintained by many high authorities, against whom the charge of rationalism cannot be urged.[2] The sweet honey-like taste, the whitish colour, the similarity of the name, and the fact that it must be collected before sunrise, after which time it hardens, or altogether dis-

[1] It was in this monastery that Tischendorf discovered in 1844 some fragments of an ancient Greek MS. of the Bible. In 1859, travelling under the patronage of the Emperor of Russia, he was presented with the priceless treasure of the Codex Sinaiticus, the oldest extant MS. of the New Testament. Here also, in 1892, the now famous Sinai Palimpsest was discovered.

[2] For a very elaborate and able discussion of the whole subject, see Ritter's *Geography of Palestine and the Sinaitic Peninsula* (vol. ii. pp. 271–292).

appears, have been adduced in proof of this conclusion. But the preponderance of opinion is on the other side, and in favour of the view that the manna was not merely increased, but absolutely produced by miracle.

The various legendary marvels which the monks here, as everywhere throughout the East, have accumulated around their convent, need not detain us long. A glance will suffice for the tomb of St. Catherine and the shrine of the Burning Bush—the bush still growing out of the soil! All our interest is concentrated upon the one great event of the desert, the manifestation of the Deity to Moses and the camp of Israel. The traditional peak is Jebel Mûsa, which rises to the height of 2,600 feet above the convent, 7,375 above the level of the sea. There are two roads to the summit. One, constructed some years ago by Abba Pasha, winds round the mountains and is available for camels. The old road is much rougher and steeper, but is far more interesting. Ascending by the former, a gradual slope leads upward for some distance from the convent for about two hours. Here a curious basin hollowed out of the rock is shown as the footprint of Mohammed's camel! From this point the track becomes narrower and steeper, in one place passing through a narrow gap between granite rocks only a few feet wide. A flight of rude stone steps now conducts to the actual summit, where a Christian church and a Mohammedan mosque stand side by side. The view is grand and impressive, ranging over a vast chaos of bare desolate peaks; but it is difficult to convince oneself that this can be the scene of the giving of the law. No plain is visible in which the tribes could have encamped in the " wilderness before the mount." The Wâdy Sebâiyeh has been pointed out as answering to the requirements of the narrative, but it is too narrow and restricted in area, too rough and boulder-strewn, to have answered the purpose.

Descending by the steeper and older road, we pass, not far from the summit, a magnificent cypress tree towering up amongst the rocks. This is alleged to mark the spot where the Lord appeared to Elijah in fire and storm and earthquake, and spoke to him in " a still small voice." [1] Close by it is a chapel dedicated to the prophet, and said to be built over the cave to which he had retired. Leaving the plateau on which the chapel stands, we make our way through a narrow path in the rocks, over a flight of rugged broken steps, the road twisting through clefts and chasms and under crags in a bewildering manner, till we come suddenly upon a remarkable archway constructed of blocks of granite. Here, and at another similar archway a little lower down, the monks used to stand to shrive and absolve the pilgrims on their ascent, before they were permitted to tread the holy ground. Various legendary shrines and a spring of deliciously clear cold water, encircled by a luxuriant growth of maiden-hair ferns, are passed in the steep descent, and at length the convent is safely reached.

Rejecting the claims of Serbal and of Jebel Mûsa to be regarded as the Mountain of the Law, the question recurs—can any peak be pointed out which does fully and completely satisfy the requirements of the narrative ? There can, I think, be no doubt as to the answer. We have but to re-ascend the mountain as far as the chapel of Elijah, and then, instead of climbing to the peak of Jebel Mûsa, bear away to the north-west over some broken

[1] 1 Kings xix.

ground and through a series of ravines to reach the summit of Râs Sufsâfeh. Here the great plain of Er-Râhah stretches away immediately below us, affording ample space for the hosts of Israel to encamp, whilst the mountain is exposed to view from summit to base. The narrative, if read from this point, becomes perfectly clear. Each detail in the text finds its corresponding feature in the landscape. Every traveller admits that, if this be not the Mountain of the Law, no other spot can be found more suitable in every respect.[1]

EGYPT, SINAI, CANAAN! The typical and spiritual significance of the histories which these names embody, have been perceived by the Church in every age. Volumes have been written to illustrate and enforce the lessons taught us by the House of Bondage, the Miraculous Deliverance, the Wilderness of Wandering, the Mountain of the Law, and the Promised Land. May we lay to heart one of these lessons inculcated by inspired teaching :

" Ye are not come unto the mount that might be touched, and that burned with fire, nor unto blackness, and darkness, and tempest, and the sound of a trumpet, and the voice of words ; which voice they that heard

---

[1] Mr. C. T. Currelly, in Chapter XVI. of Petrie's *Researches in Sinai*, makes the following statement as to the suitability of Er Raha to be the scene of the encampment of the Israelites under Moses : " I do not think it is possible to keep a people through a winter on the plain of Er Raha. One night when we were there the water in our tanks froze to the depth of an inch, and in spite of our heavy clothes we suffered considerably, and our men were badly exhausted with the extreme cold. . . . I do not think anybody would wish to postulate an alteration in temperature, and women and children could not live in this plain without such a change." His judgment is in favour of the Wâdy Feiran as the scene of the encampment, and Serbal as the Mount of the Law.

intreated that the word should not be spoken to them any more : . . . but ye are come unto Mount Sion, and unto the city of the living God, the heavenly Jerusalem, and to an innumerable company of angels, to the general assembly and church of the firstborn, which are written in heaven, and to God the Judge of all, and to the spirits of just men made perfect, and to Jesus the mediator of the new covenant, and to the blood of sprinkling, that speaketh better things than that of Abel. See that ye refuse not Him that speaketh. For if they escaped not who refused Him that spake on earth, much more shall not we escape, if we turn away from Him that speaketh from heaven." [1]

[1] Hebrews xii. 18–25.

INDEX